Tuesday

A young girl sits alo... ...s.
Her soldier boyfrien... ... ‐
vice abroad. What ha... ...t
ninety minutes chan... ...r
father, war and viole..., ...

Tuesday was commissioned by the BBC Schools Service and televised for 14- to 17-year-olds.

This volume contains the original text – also suitable for the stage – a poem and stories used in rehearsals for *Tuesday*, and comprehensive teaching notes, including an interview with the playwright.

Edward Bond was born and educated in London. His plays include *The Pope's Wedding* (Royal Court Theatre, 1962), *Saved* (Royal Court, 1965), *Early Morning* (Royal Court, 1968), *Narrow Road to the Deep North* (Belgrade Theatre, Coventry, 1968; Royal Court, 1969), *Black Mass* (Sharpeville Commemoration Evening, Lyceum Theatre, 1970), *Passion* (CND Rally, Alexandra Palace, 1971), *Lear* (Royal Court, 1971), *The Sea* (Royal Court, 1973), *Bingo* (Northcott, Exeter, 1973; Royal Court, 1974), *The Fool* (Royal Court, 1975), *The Bundle* (RSC Warehouse, 1978), *The Woman* (National Theatre, 1978), *The Worlds* (New Half Moon Theatre, London, 1981), *Restoration* (Royal Court, 1981), *Summer* (National Theatre, 1982), *Derek* (RSC Youth Festival, The Other Place, Stratford-upon-Avon, 1982), *The Cat* (produced in Germany as *The English Cat* by the Stuttgart Opera, 1983), *Human Cannon* (Quantum Theatre, Manchester, 1986), *The War Plays* (*Red Black and Ignorant*, *The Tin Can People* and *Great Peace*) which were staged as a trilogy by the RSC at the Barbican Pit in 1985, *Jackets* (Leicester Haymarket, 1989), *September* (Canterbury Cathedral, 1989), *In the Company of Men* (Paris, 1992), *Olly's Prison* (BBC 2 Television 1993), *Tuesday* (BBC Schools TV, 1993). His *Theatre Poems and Songs* were published in 1978 and *Poems 1978–1985* in 1987.

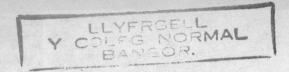

Edward Bond

Tuesday

with full teaching notes and an interview with the author
by Jim Mulligan

METHUEN DRAMA

METHUEN MODERN PLAYS

First published in Great Britain 1993
by Methuen Drama
an imprint of Reed Consumer Books Ltd
Michelin House, 81 Fulham Road, London SW3 6RB
and Auckland, Melbourne, Singapore and Toronto

ISBN 0–413–68220-X

A CIP catalogue record for this book
is available at the British Library

Typeset by Hewer Text Composition Services, Edinburgh
Printed in Great Britain by Cox and Wyman Ltd, Reading, Berks

Front cover photograph of Natalie Morse as Irene.
Photo by Luke Finn, copyright © BBC Education

Contents

Tuesday 1

The Rehearsals 39
The Dramatic Child 42
Famine 51

Interview and Teaching Notes 53

Interview with Edward Bond 54

Teaching Notes 61
  What's it all about? 61
  Peeling the Onion: layers of meaning 62
  Paths to production 64
  'The Plastic Water Bottle' 66
  Every word you choose, every phrase you use:
    the drafting process 70
  Ideas for writing 74
  Just when you thought you had finished . . . 75

Tuesday

Tuesday was first broadcast by BBC Education in March 1993, with the following cast:

FATHER	Bob Peck
BRIAN	Ben Chaplin
IRENE	Natalie Morse
FIRST PC	Che Walker
SECOND PC	Matthew Lloyd Lewis
THIRD PC	Niall Refoy
SENIOR OFFICER	Richard Cubison
NEIGHBOUR	Tracie Hart
MEDIC	Colin Bourner
CHILD	Elliot Henderson-Boyle

Produced by	Richard Langridge
Directed by	Edward Bond
	Sharon Miller

Tuesday was commissioned by BBC TV Education and first broadcast in three weekly parts. These parts are shown in this script. But as the play occurs in 'real time' – the time is continuous – it need not be divided into separate parts.

The play may be staged in this version. No interval would be necessary but there could be one at or a little before the ending of Part Two.

When the play was filmed the police and medics were used in an elaborate way. They could be staged more simply. It depends on the nature of the production – for example on the number of players and amount of equipment available.

Setting

A small upstairs bedroom in a suburban pre-war house converted to flats. A window. Outside it the roofs of the houses and factories in a light industrial suburb. When the brick-red window curtains are drawn light filters through the material. On the wall, two posters or unframed prints and a framed picture of Colley Wood, showing the sea seen through trees. A free-standing wardrobe – a dress hangs on the outside on a clothes-hanger. A neatly made single bed with a middling-to-dark blue coverlet. Slippers by the bed. Below the window a chair and table used as a dressing-table and a desk. On the table some test exam papers, a few reference books, a plastic ruler, a green eraser and a ceramic pot holding five or six biros and pencils.

for Richard Langridge

PART ONE

IRENE *sits in a chair at the desk. She is in her mid-teens. She wears a skirt, blouse and an open cardigan. She is answering questions in a set of test exam papers. She is lost in thought as she considers which question to answer next. Then she begins to write, looking slightly sideways at the ball of the biro. Silence except for* IRENE's *hand on the paper. A doorbell rings downstairs.* IRENE *ignores it and goes on writing. The doorbell rings again. After a moment's pause she makes a small sound of annoyance and goes on writing. Pause.*

IRENE (*calls*). Dad.

A moment's silence and then the doorbell again – a long persistent ring. Without changing her expression or making a sound IRENE *stops writing, puts down her biro and goes out. She leaves the door open.*

Silence. The sound of four feet running upstairs.

(*Off.*) Who said you could go up!

BRIAN *comes in, followed by* IRENE. *He is in his late teens. He has short hair and wears dark jeans and a dark wind-cheater over a shirt.*

You've got leave! Why didn't you phone! (*She puts her arms round him.*) You want to surprise me!

BRIAN *leaves* IRENE *and shuts the door.*

Dad'll be back.

BRIAN *goes to the bed and sits on the side.*

What is it? Something's the matter.

BRIAN *looks at her a moment.*

BRIAN. Done a runner.
IRENE. Oh. (*Slight pause.*) You've run away?
BRIAN. Yes.
IRENE. Why? Have you done something to . . .?

BRIAN (*violently*). No no! (*Immediately:*) *I've* done something! What chance –! How can you make anyone understand? *I* haven't done it! It's not me!

IRENE *stares at him.*

(*Calmer.*) I ran. That's all.

IRENE. Why?

BRIAN. You've got to hide me.

IRENE. Hide you? (*Bewildered.*) What've you done? This is stupid –

BRIAN. I told you I –

IRENE (*suddenly trying to take control*). What's happened? Did they do something to you? What? (*Sudden idea.*) Are they following you?

BRIAN. You've got to hide me. There's nowhere else now.

IRENE. But they'll come here. Dad'll be back – any minute . . . (*Tries to think.*) Do your people know you're –?

BRIAN. No no. I didn't go there. They wouldn't hide me.

IRENE. The army'll go there. They'll give them our name. The army'll go everywhere you're known. They could be –

BRIAN. No – they don't know I've run. This morning – I walked out the barracks. I won't be missed yet.

IRENE. Then you can go back – if you've done nothing to –

BRIAN. No.

IRENE. Why not? (*Idea.*) Was there a fight?

BRIAN. Nothing, nothing happened. Let me stay. Tell the police you haven't seen me.

IRENE (*trying to understand*). You've run away. Are you hurt?

BRIAN *turns and lies face down on the bed.*

BRIAN. No. Tired.

IRENE (*stares at him*). If they've done something to you – you mustn't run away – you'll put yourself in the wrong.

BRIAN (*face down on the bed*). I ask for help – isn't that enough? . . . Help me.

IRENE. I am helping. Why've you run away? (*No answer.*) Let me phone the barracks – the welfare. I'll tell them you're ill. It's not helping you if I let you get into – I'll tell them *I'm* ill. You stayed to help me to . . .

BRIAN (*face down*). I'm not going back.

IRENE. They'll come and take you back.

BRIAN (*low*). They may. They can. (*Into the blankets.*) But I won't go. I won't *turn* in that direction. Never. (*Small and intense.*) They'll have to turn the world round so the barrack's facing me . . . I could lie here. Be asleep. Dream it out. Make sense.

IRENE. You can't stay even if I said you could. You can't just vanish! Dad's coming. The neighbours would see you at the windows. They know you. If you're running away you have to go further than this. God knows where! (*No answer.*) This is silly.

BRIAN. Then I can stay for a while? That's what you meant, I heard you. Let me stay. I can think here.

IRENE. You can't think! If you could you'd tell me what happened. The police'll tell me their version – not yours.

BRIAN. It doesn't matter. They couldn't understand if I told them. If they'd been there they wouldn't even have seen it.

IRENE *draws the curtains.*

IRENE. I'll have to manage. I'll try.

BRIAN *turns to face her.*

BRIAN. I knew you'd let me.

IRENE (*pause*). D'you want a drink?

BRIAN. Not yet. (*Silence.*) The army doesn't know. No one does. Perhaps no one ever will. Or I'll wait for years and tell a stranger. No – it'd be too late. It's too late now. If I told anyone – and they couldn't understand – jeered – I wouldn't want to live. Not even with you.

IRENE. I won't jeer.

BRIAN. No no, you wouldn't. That's strange. Being understood would be even worse than not being understood – in this world.

IRENE (*not understanding*). Worse? (*Frightened.*) Is it me?

What have I done? (*Tries to think.*) Did I hurt anyone by –
was it my letters? Tell me! – why are you here?

BRIAN. When I ran away this morning, I meant to go absent
for a few days. Get drunk – spew it out of me – then go back
like a corpse with a hangover. They'd welcome me with
open arms – one of the lads had proved he rated! Now I
can't. It's you. If I told you, you wouldn't let me go back. I
know. (*Touches the bed at his side.*) Trust me.

IRENE (*doesn't move*). What am I being blamed for?

BRIAN. It's not blame. I don't know what it is. It must be
thanks. I can't tell you – I can't hurt you. Because you're
kind. (*Suddenly his mind drifts.*) Orders, orders. The army's
always giving orders. They'd give orders to the hairs on a
toothbrush.

IRENE *turns to the door, unsure.*

IRENE. Was that a key?

BRIAN *stands. Listens. Tense. Pause. He shakes his head.*

He went to the job centre. He should be back.

BRIAN (*flat*). Perhaps he got an interview. (*He sits at the
table.*) You were studying. Go on – don't let me hold you
up.

IRENE. Go on? You come here – do this – and tell me to go
on as if –

BRIAN. Why not? It's just thinking and writing it on paper.
(*Silence.*) A fly knows more about death than we do. When
you could die any second, you don't pray. You loot instead.
So you've got something to take home. You rob the dead to
show your guts still want you to live. God doesn't help you,
the dead do. Perhaps they pity you because you're alive. I
got an officer's pistol. Inlaid.

IRENE (*quietly*). The fighting's over. They can't send you
back now you're home. You're not running from that.

BRIAN. I'm not running. It's more serious: I walked . . . I
left so quietly my shadow's still back there looking for me.

Downstairs the sound of a door opening and closing.

FATHER (*off*). Home!

BRIAN. Don't tell him. I'll hide – (*Bed.*) under there! I won't be any –! He doesn't come in here to –

IRENE. Hide?

BRIAN. I'll be quiet. Really. I'm trained.

FATHER. (*off.*) Is the kettle on?

BRIAN *tries to hide under the bed – it is too low.*
IRENE *stares at him in astonishment.*

IRENE. You can't hide! In this flat? You'd have to stop breathing! Be invisible!

BRIAN. I don't want him here! I don't want his questions! It's your room! You promised! He won't know – he doesn't come in here!

IRENE. He's my father. It's his house.

IRENE *goes out and leaves the door open.* BRIAN *goes to it, pulls it almost shut, listens at the crack. Then he shuts it and goes to the bed. He unzips his windcheater and takes out an officer's elegant, inlaid pistol. He hides it under the pillows. He sits at the desk. Stands. Sits on the bed.*

A quiet tap on the door.

Slight pause before it opens. FATHER *pops his head and shoulders in. He is a bit thin but muscular. His face is boney, his eyebrows are a shade too thick, his hair is stubby. He wears slacks and a thickish jumper. He often jokes but has absolutely no sense of humour.*

FATHER. All right if I . . .? (*He comes in and shuts the door behind him. He speaks calmly and gently.*) Son what a surprise. Hello hello. Good to see you. Always. I told you to treat this place like home. Let's see you. (*He opens the curtains.*) That's better. Help yourself to the daylight: it's freebies. (*Turns to* BRIAN.) Oh it's you! I thought it was her other one! – Now what's all this about? Rene's got hold of some cock-'n'-bull story. You want to tell me? Take your time. Thank God you had the sense to come here and not somewhere else. We'll soon sort it out between us. Two heads eh? (*Pause*.) Job centre. You've got problems? Aaahhh. I don't know. Leak with a hole in it. The pits – wouldn't bury a dog in it if it'd bit me leg off. Come on lad – you're not getting yourself in trouble while I'm here. I'm too fond of you for that.

BRIAN. I told her not to tell you.

FATHER (*mock surprise*). Not tell Dad? She's supposed to hide you under the bed? You have to get her to sweep it first! We're not thinking straight are we? If you're in trouble that's no reason to drag her in.

IRENE *opens the door and stands in the doorway.*

Irene wait downstairs.

IRENE. I wanted to see if he's –

FATHER. Wait down like a good girl. I'll handle this. I'll bring him down in a couple of shakes.

IRENE *goes.*

FATHER (*shouts down through the open door*). I brought some shopping in. There's some stuff to go in the freezer. I couldn't get your yoghurt – I found something else. (*He shuts the door and turns to* BRIAN.) I can see you're upset. You don't have to tell me the ins and outs. I'll need to know – I'm curious anyway – but that can wait. The main thing's to catch it before it goes out of our hands. Rene says you went over the wall this morning? Right? So there's no great harm done so far. You went on a bender – young lad letting off steam – celebrate coming home in one piece – soon as you came round you reported back to the guardhouse. They'll understand – you'll be surprised. You'll lose a few weeks' wages. Finished. The family opposite've got a car. I'll borrow that and run you back. I'll pay for the petrol.

BRIAN. I have to talk to Irene.

FATHER. Yes Dad thank you very much. Why? You mean, to say goodbye?

BRIAN. You interrupted us – I hadn't finished.

FATHER. Oh dear I am sorry. Look lad I'm being patient

with you. I don't think you appreciate your situation. You're not talking to Rene – even in my presence. I wouldn't even countenance it. You're not involving a girl her age. What sort of a father would I be if I encouraged you to do that? If I can't help you, I can look after her.

BRIAN. Five minutes. That's all I need to –

FATHER. No. You can tell me anything you've got to say. I'll pass it on if I consider it's appropriate. You're not hiding behind her. You've already managed to upset her once. That's why she defied me just now in the doorway. How d'you expect her to get ready for her exams in that state? If she messes them up her whole future's put in jeopardy. She'll know who to blame then. Now you show a bit of responsibility.

BRIAN. I'll go.

FATHER. No you won't. I'm not letting you run away from this – you're starting to make a habit of it. I want to know what's going on. In this country we don't walk in and out of people's houses just as we please. I'm not just her father. I'm a member of the public. It's my responsibility to know who we're letting loose on our streets. You tell me what you're playing at.

BRIAN *goes to the door, opens it and calls down.*

BRIAN. Rene!

Calmly FATHER *reaches past* BRIAN, *pulls the door to till only a crack is open and shouts through it.*

FATHER. Stay down there! I'm not playing about! I don't want you up here – it's bad enough with him! (FATHER *closes the door and turns to* BRIAN.) Look lad. We'll start again. I'm trying to be your friend but you're not making it easy. I can't help you if you won't tell me what you've done.

BRIAN. I'm sorry I got you into this. I'll –

FATHER. Don't be sorry! I don't mind, it's my job! Haven't you got that in your nut yet? Look. The fighting upset you – them killing your mates – you killing them back. I know all about it. I was in the army. It's worse for someone like you. You're a considerate lad – good heart – that's why Rene took you up. (*No response.*) Worse than that is it? Something happened when you were out there – and you chickened out: now the lads are ganging up on you? Well – fine. You ran in the heat of the moment. Nothing to be ashamed of – better men than you have done it. But if you run now – when you're with friends trying to help – then you've got a hard life ahead of you. (*Pause.*) I see. It's as bad as that is it? – the officers. If you're being victimised I'll be the first to stand up for you. You go back and hand yourself in – if you don't play by the rules you get nowhere – but there are crowds of people out there waiting to rally round and help. We'll fight your corner. It's a free country – wasn't that why you were fighting? We can take it to our MP if we have to! (*No response.*) Your behaviour's telling me you don't trust me lad. I'm sorry.

BRIAN *tries to go to the door.* FATHER *blocks his way.*

BRIAN (*flat*). Please. Let me go.
FATHER (*low*). Are you threatening me son?
BRIAN. Let me go.
FATHER. I don't know, there's some funny people about. He comes to my house. Invites himself upstairs. Upsets my daughter. Threatens me. Then when he doesn't get it all his own way he thinks he can walk off without so much as a by your leave. This is your prison. That door's shut till I say sesame (it happens to speak my language). Right, we've had our bit of fun. Now I'm telling you, not asking. I want to know what your game is. You could've murdered someone – put some old woman in hospital. You did *some*thing to get yourself in this state! The way you're carrying on isn't much of an assurance. If I let you through that door that makes me an accomplice of God knows –
BRIAN. No one knows I was here.
FATHER. My daughter knows. Am I supposed to lie in front of her? – your idea of a father-daughter relationship? Lad the more you say the less I like to hear. You always were a

step out of line. She can't say I didn't warn her. Now, shall I call the police? They won't be so patient.

BRIAN *goes to the bed and sits on the side.*

BRIAN. I can't tell you.

FATHER. Oh? Why?

BRIAN. You wouldn't understand.

FATHER. Oh – I'm stupid? I don't believe I'm hearing this! You can tell my daughter – she's not stupid? It's Sonny Jim against the rest of the world!

BRIAN. I can't. I'm sorry. I don't know how. I can't make you understand. I wish I could!

FATHER *sits on the bed beside* BRIAN.

FATHER. You youngsters. All this fuss! In the end it's all nothing. The states Irene gets into – God knows why! I wish you'd trust me. I could have it all wrapped up by now. Finished and done with . . . I'm sorry I shouted. You don't need that. Sometimes it all gets on top. You'll know, when it's your turn. No work. The house needs attention. I'd like to afford Irene a few extras – some fun with her mates. Get her nose out of her books for a while. She's a good girl.

BRIAN. I can't.

FATHER. Now I'll tell you things you've never heard me talk about. Secrets I keep from Irene. I've seen it. Tanks on fire. Human ovens. Legs and arms sticking out the turrets – waving about – like the legs of a beetle on its back. They were dead – bodies contracting in the heat. We called it the fire dance. They didn't feel it but we had to see it. A cannibal would walk away from that with my blessing . . . You're in a state of shock. I can see it. Ill. That's why you've got to go to the authorities. If you cut your finger you go and get it bound up. That's what authority's for. You don't start barging into little girls' rooms and telling them the world doesn't understand you (*Sigh.*) – if you do that you'll be in very deep water my friend. I'll call the police – for your own sake. If you've got anything to say to

me say it before – (*Stops, puzzled. Stares at* BRIAN.) What
is it?

BRIAN (*starts to laugh*). . . . the turrets . . .

FATHER (*gently, hand on* BRIAN's *arm*). I'm sorry you take
the –

BRIAN. Don't. (*He stands.*) Don't! Questions! Questions!
Prying! You're not happy till you get to – find someone
suffering! What made you like that? You've no right to
question me!

FATHER (*low threat*). Don't look at me like that. No right? –
in my house! No right! If you look at me like that I'll put
your eyes out! My God I'm not a man of violence! I could
take you outside and give you the thrashing of your life!
You couldn't run anywhere, you couldn't crawl! You're
younger than me, but what I feel now – I'd put you down!
. . . I didn't know I could be so angry! What right've you
got to upset me? Did I come here with accusations? I
offered help! D'you think I'll go down on my knees?
Prying? He comes in here taking over my house! I don't
care what you've done! I wouldn't listen if you told me!
You're not important enough to bother with! Keep your
grubby little secret! You're a coward! – that's what you
can't tell!

The door opens and IRENE *comes in.*

I told you to wait down there!

IRENE *goes to* BRIAN.

BRIAN (*to* FATHER). I can't tell you! (*To* IRENE.) How
can I tell it here – to a man like that! In this room – it
doesn't make sense!

FATHER. (*to* IRENE). Go down! (*To* BRIAN.) What's
wrong with the room? My God – he doesn't like the
wallpaper! He doesn't like me – the way I live – he doesn't
like anything! (*To* IRENE.) Go! He was going to tell me – I
had him there – and you barge in!

BRIAN. Let her alone! You make it worse! – everything you
do! If I wanted to tell you I couldn't now! Look – no one

else knows I'm here! I won't tell! Is that what you're afraid
of? You're in the clear with the —
FATHER. I beg your pardon? In the clear? I *am* in the clear
lad! Don't patronise *me*! I don't need assurances from you!
BRIAN (*to* IRENE). You told *him*? Trusted *him*?
FATHER. Now start on her! Get one thing straight: I'm
answerable to no one in this house! What I do in this place
is right because I say so! Oh I'm not letting a little
runaway-sneak like you upset me. I said I'd help you
and I will! I keep my word! It's time you were taught a
lesson! When you leave this house the police'll be on your
tail. Then God help you!
IRENE (*to* BRIAN). You must tell us! There must be
something if it causes all this trouble even before we know
what it is! The police will come — and if there's something
that should be done, we can't do it . . . it'll be too late . . .

FATHER *goes to the door and opens it.*

FATHER. Take my advice and move! I'm calling them.
IRENE. No! He must tell us what happened!
FATHER. Nothing happened! (*To* BRIAN.) You've run into
something you can't push out of your way! It's all right
Irene. He saw a few bodies — a *lot*! — saw them dying! (*He
half turns to* BRIAN.) I'm not the fool he thinks I am. I
know what he means about this room. You don't talk about
that here. One day you find yourself somewhere counting
bodies. Well — *someone* wants to know. He wants to go on
counting marbles! Play truant from war! (*To* BRIAN.)
What about the other lads? Did they run? They didn't
like it any more than you. Some of them are dead because
you ran! My God if those lads were out there I'd have to
stop them getting at you! (*He is standing in the open
doorway. He bangs his fist on the outside of the door.*) That's
them! Trying to get in! (*He bangs on the door. He pretends to
shout to soldiers in the corridor.*) All right lads I'll fix him!
(*To* BRIAN.) They're not a pretty sight! (*He comes into the
room.*) I'm not leaving you with my daughter! Get down
there!

BRIAN *takes the gun from under the pillow. He holds it up but does not aim it directly at* FATHER.

(*Jeering in fear.*) . . . Oh put it away sonny. You don't know what you're doing. Now he's got his toys out . . .

BRIAN (*shuts the door*). . . . Oh Christ I didn't want it . . .

FATHER. (*his fear becomes real.*) Put it down son. Put it down. You don't mean it. That's right – you don't want to harm –

BRIAN. Why did he bang on the door! Who are you to let people in and out just because they're dead.

FATHER (*mumbles in panic*). He's mad he's mad oh God why did I try to help the –

BRIAN. The keeper of the door! Don't call me lad! I'm not your son!

FATHER. If there was some other way to bring children into the world we would take the care of – please please don't lad – sir – you're harming yourself by – son I –

BRIAN. Son! Son! He's said it again! If I was your father son! – I'd tell you! – everything! I'd teach you your first word! Say it – say it – after me! *Sorry*! Say it!

FATHER. Sorry, sorry sorry for everything you – talk to me – I want to help . . . (*Tearful grin.*) . . . Oh is this a game? . . . (*To* IRENE.) You're in it too . . .!

BRIAN. The keeper of the door! He saw the dead! In tanks! Dancing!

FATHER (*panic whisper*). A madman in our house – shut in with a –

BRIAN. Get down! Get down! (FATHER *paralysed.*) I told you to get down!

Suddenly FATHER *scuttles to the door.* BRIAN *half trips him.*

No! No! (*Points to floor.*) Down! Down! You don't get out of it now.

FATHER *drops to his knees.*

(*Eyes closed.*) Dance. Like the men in the tank. The keeper of the door. Show me. How they danced in the turret.

Pause.

FATHER. Err – I – (*He is making a few vague gestures with his hands.*) Sorry.

BRIAN *has opened his eyes. He stares at* FATHER.

BRIAN. . . . the pity of it . . . yes . . .

IRENE *goes to* FATHER *and helps him to his feet.*

IRENE. Get up – you've done enough – there's no need now . . .

FATHER *head bowed, cringes away from her.*

FATHER . . . he'll shoot me with his . . . (*Pushes her away.*) . . . no no the man will shoot us with the . . . all the people he . . .

IRENE. Stand up. (*Lifts* FATHER *to his feet.*) There. No one will hurt you. (*She turns to* BRIAN.) Give it to me.

BRIAN. Yes . . . take it – take it . . . Let's be at peace.

BRIAN *gives her the gun. She goes to the desk and sits with it in her lap. Silence.*

FATHER (*low*). Ha!

Silence.

FATHER *starts to jab the air with his finger. A hollow laugh with each jab.*

Ha! Ha! Ha! Ha! Ha! (*Leans against wall.*) A little girl asks – he . . .

Hollow laugh – he sidles with his back along the wall. IRENE *stands.*

Hahahahahahaha! . . . he gives it! Ha! Ha! Ha! (*Brushes against a picture on the wall, straightens it with one hand.*) The coward afraid what comes – next! Can't go that far! Took in by my little wheeze! Didn't know – took him for a ride! (*Points a finger at the picture.*) 'Colley Wood: A View of the Sea.' (*Suddenly waves his arms as if he's frightening a*

child by pretending to be a ghoul.) Oooh! On the run! The
only place he runs is in his jeans! It isn't ended, isn't ended!
(*He picks up the chair and poses with it menacingly over his
head*.) Wouldn't tell? I know now! – what I need! He drew a
gun! With witnesses! (*To* IRENE.) Go down! Get the
police! In the street! (*Calls*.) Police! (*To* BRIAN, *still
holding the chair as before*.) Stay there! No pity now! It's
gone!

IRENE. There's no need for the rest.

FATHER *sharp, jerks head*.

FATHER. What?

IRENE. He came. You came, I came . . . He didn't hurt us
. . . If we knew what we're doing in this room. (*Looks at the
exam papers*.) They want these in the morning. (*To*
BRIAN.) Why can't you tell us what happened? Why
not? At least say that.

BRIAN *has slumped onto the bed*. FATHER *still stands with
the chair over his head*.

FATHER (*laugh*). Write it. Pen and paper.

IRENE. I'll go with you.

FATHER. No you can't. The exams are coming. He'll leave
you. Get you into trouble.

IRENE (*to* BRIAN). How much money have you got?

No answer.

FATHER. You can't. He doesn't want you. Tell her! It's not
the money! He'd batter some old woman – take you to a
Chinese take-away to celebrate!

IRENE. My father hides his money in his room. I'll steal it.

FATHER. Ha! He's lost his voice – makes a habit! It's the
next day now, the morning after! He doesn't want you!
Pathetic little tart! . . . My daughter's a tart! I'll give him
that: he's got his head screwed on. Wouldn't shoot me: too
messy! Wouldn't take you: cramp his style! See what he is!
You'd go with that? See him! Give him the gun!

FATHER *puts down the chair, goes to the wall and turns his face to it.*

IRENE *sits in the chair.*

Shoot me! I've turned my back! Made it easy! Look – I've got a blindfold!

FATHER *puts the crook of his arm over his eyes, still facing the wall.*

IRENE *and* BRIAN *do not move.*

Take the gun! He can't! I could stand here till I drop dead! He can't!
IRENE (*to* FATHER). Don't do it!
FATHER (*as before, squinting out from under his arm*). I give the order: shoot!
IRENE. Leave him alone. (*Very low.*) Leave yourself alone.
FATHER (*turns to* IRENE, *exultant*). I've never been so safe! I feel it! Every pore!

In the chair, IRENE *raises the gun – it points at* FATHER.

IRENE. Now yes.

IRENE *pulls the trigger: click. Silence.*

FATHER (*too stunned to finish*). She –

IRENE *gets up from the chair. She takes a few steps towards* FATHER. *She is holding out the gun with one hand. The gun shakes violently. She holds it with both hands. The shaking becomes slower but more pronounced. She aims at* FATHER. *He crouches, draws in his breath – almost too high to be heard.*

IRENE *pulls the trigger three times: click – click – click. The gun stops shaking.*

IRENE. It doesn't work.

FATHER *scampers across the floor to* BRIAN, *grabs his legs.*

FATHER (*like a baby being sick*). She tried to –

IRENE (*like a small child*). It didn't go – I didn't –

BRIAN *goes to* IRENE. FATHER *clings and scuttles along behind him.* BRIAN *takes the gun from* IRENE – *she doesn't resist.* FATHER *scuttles away from* BRIAN – *backs away to the wall.*

FATHER (*terrified giggle, head in hands*). I can't – any more –
BRIAN (*holding out the gun*). It's not loaded.

BRIAN *puts the gun on the desk.*

FATHER *sways to the desk like a cripple. He accidentally knocks a few exam papers to the floor. He picks up the gun, tries to look at it, drops it to the floor. He falls against the desk.*

BRIAN. Brought it to scare anyone who . . . I'd never kill . . . No bullets – so I'd never be in the situation of . . .
FATHER. Did she know? Did she know?

IRENE *walks to the table.* FATHER *flinches away as she passes.*

(*Flat whine.*) She's got a knife.

IRENE *picks up the fallen exam papers. She lays them on the table without sorting them.*

IRENE (*looking at the sheaf of papers*). Sometimes there's a terrible tragedy. You have to play your part.

PART TWO

FATHER *and* BRIAN *stare at* IRENE. *She stares down blankly at the exam papers.*

FATHER. She tried to kill me.

BRIAN. She didn't.

FATHER. My daughter tried to . . . !

BRIAN. It wasn't loaded – she saw. It's my fault. I brought the gun.

FATHER. I could be dead. (*He stares at* IRENE, *then turns to* BRIAN.) Yes your fault! You've done this! You didn't tell . . . ! I never rowed like – we treated each other with respect. Human beings – not animals, criminals! (*He points to the gun on the floor.*) Put it away! Get rid of it!

BRIAN *picks up the gun.*

She stood there and tried to . . . What am I going to do? I can't live with her here. I can never trust her after what happened in this room. Every cup of tea – I'd wonder what she'd put in it. This isn't my house any more. (*Starts to go.*)

BRIAN. Where are you going?

FATHER. To be sick. Is that all right? I have to be in this house with filth – at least let me sick it out of my body!

He goes.

IRENE. I don't understand how it happened.

BRIAN. When the police come I'll hand myself in. What else? Everywhere's like this. I'm – I'm no good at living. I ask too much – and that's too little. Why did you do that to him?

IRENE. You made him crawl . . . !

BRIAN. It was a trick – scare him – tie him up – get away – (*Stops.*) I knew it wasn't loaded. He knew – in the back of his mind – I didn't mean to kill him. I couldn't fake that. No one can. I saw squaddies' faces when they killed. It was on your face. If the gun had been loaded he . . . You were lucky. It's all over. I'm like him. I can't live with you now.

That's what you've turned me into. When you're shot you don't have time to hear the gun. You're dead too soon. You don't even feel the bullet. You're too shocked by what's on the killer's face. You're looking into hell. So you think you're already dead and in hell forever. That's how they spent their last seconds. Without hope. You went one better. You made him stare at your face while you fumbled with the trigger. He's trying to sick your face up. He won't. You've tattooed it on his brain.

IRENE. You said you meant to go back – till you saw me. What did I do?

BRIAN. No, forget it. It's all changed. I'm going back. Think of what you did to *him*.

IRENE. I want to know. What does it matter to you now you're going back?

BRIAN. Everyone's in a room like this. I don't know how we live in it. I'll tell you. I want to know if you can still understand. It's not much of a story. It was in the desert. A temporary hold-up. A few days quiet before the order to go in. Even in war you can slip away. I took a walk in no man's land. The dunes. Covered in long neat rows of little waves. Beautiful. Then where they were slashed open by tanks. Machines dragging their graves behind them. I passed there and went on. It was still. Flat. Sand. Flatter than the sky. I saw – how far? – a shadow. Black. Dot. A periscope sticking up from a secret dug-out? No it was a moving shadow. First I didn't see the thing that made it. Lost in the heat. Then I saw something white. Walking on the shadow. A mirage? In war you're in the mirage. I got closer. A man. A dwarf. Walking on its own shadow. I should've turned back. Against orders being there. You must see everything, it's not given to you again. A little chap walking away. The shadow round its feet. Five? Six? It wore a white thing. I thought I was silent in the sand. Sand must make many sounds. He knew them all. It was a different place for him. He turned and looked straight over his shoulder. *At* me. No expression – but he saw. I couldn't shout. I was afraid the sand would hear me and try to bury

me. I pointed my gun. What else could I do? Not in anger.
It was a pointed finger made of metal. He looked over his
shoulder and went on. Didn't hurry. His face didn't
change. I don't know if he was calm. I ran. Fell. The
sand was ice to me. I slid – digging in – trying to get to my
feet. In my eyes and mouth and collar. That was worst. It
trickled down my back as if, as if . . . I shuddered. I
reached him. He went on. Didn't flinch or change his
line. The sand didn't hurt him – I tore it to bits just
being there. I stumbled beside him. Put out my hand. I
couldn't touch him. Speak English? Speeky Iingleesshh? I
was crying. Spitting sand. Tell me, tell me, tell me . . . He
didn't answer. He didn't have the words. He went on.
Sometimes now I speak – ordinary things. Shut the door –
more tea – and there's bits of sand in my mouth. I fell back.
Let him go. I was lost. Crying. The sand was turning to
scum – mud – on my face. He didn't look round. Went on.
He knew I couldn't hurt him. Some of our planes rose up
on the horizon and went down again. The sand was opening
out between us. A child is lifted from its mother – the cord
stretches. It walked away. From its father – mother – us.
Children are meant to cry for food. The cold. The dark.
Alone. For comfort. It walked away. From everyone. We
hate and kill. It had had enough. Children have begun to
walk away from human beings . . . I let it go – to grow up
into one of theirs to kill us. I went back to my unit. Slow –
the desert was a lump of mud stuck to my boots. We got the
order. Went to war. Killed. Then home. Bands. Streamers.
Celebrations. I can't forget the child. I went for the wrong
walk. I met myself.

IRENE. You mustn't tell my father. Please. You'd hurt
yourself. He'd never understand. It'd be one of his
jokes. It would crucify you.

BRIAN. Do *you* understand?

IRENE. Yes. You can't go back. You mustn't.

BRIAN. Ha!

IRENE. It's dangerous for you.

BRIAN. You've driven me back! When I saw you I thought:

the child could be hers. The world's okay – safe. Then you took the gun – like all the rest!

IRENE. No! It was different!

BRIAN. *How?* (*He stares at her for a moment, then turns away. Anger.*) What's it matter? I met a loony child! Food doesn't drop out of the sky just because it's in the desert! Some sappers clearing mines'll find a little skeleton with sand in its mouth.

IRENE. He's climbing up in his socks.

Silence. The door opens and FATHER *comes in. He has taken off his shoes.*

FATHER. I had a sandwich at the job centre. They've got a little caff section. Lay on my stomach. (*To* IRENE.) Sorry sorry . . . you knew it wasn't loaded . . . we're a family . . . you'd never . . . it's not possible, it doesn't happen. You pulled my leg. I was confused – worried over you lad – so I fell for it. I wish *you* were pulling my leg. But you're telling the truth. Why should you lie to me? The trouble you've got coming to you.

BRIAN. You phoned the police.

FATHER. Now now. I told you – I was sick. And I had other things to think of: I still thought Rene had tried to – (*To* IRENE.) Sorry sorry. (*To* BRIAN.) When did I have time to phone? Don't be silly.

IRENE. He's giving himself up.

FATHER. Oh? What changed your mind? (*To* IRENE.) I didn't phone. (*To* BRIAN.) How can I trust the 'latest'? You might change it again on the stairs.

IRENE. The police told you to talk to keep him here.

FATHER. I'm not repeating myself again. If you'd had the sense to tell me why you came here none of this – the row, the gun – would've happened.

BRIAN (*to* IRENE). Shall I tell him?

IRENE. No. Why waste your time? He can't understand.

FATHER. Try me.

IRENE (*to* BRIAN). Go to prison if you want. But I have to live here. I don't want to see any more. Please.

BRIAN. I must try. He must understand something. Something must get through to him. Mr Briggs – please – sit down.

FATHER. Are you going to tell me your *secret*?

BRIAN. Yes yes.

FATHER *sits on the side of the bed.*

Listen. There was a hill. They're dug in on the top. We came up firing. Mortars, grenades. Went in. Cleared it out. We were in a space – like a room – so flat you could've laid a carpet – rocks sticking up like bits left of the walls. Their dead on the floor. Their wounded shivering on the rocks. Quiet. The wounded snivelling – the odd sound of fighting – made it quieter. Fags out, lit up. Ping on the rock. We've got a sniper. Then one of theirs – wound in the gut – started to whine for mum. Same word in any language. It gets louder. One of ours – nerves gone – goes over to theirs yelling shut it, shut it – tries sign language with the bayonet. Theirs: mmeeoowwmmuummhhaaa – like a soccer chant. Ours screaming: not words now – warning – orders – reasons – praying – telling how'd-I-know? – a bedtime story to make him stop – on and on – my language – the language I dream in – this language – but I don't know it – screaming – an animal down his throat he's sicking up, it's digging down. Theirs: maahwah – maahwah – maahwah – maahwah! Ours: screaming. Theirs: maahwah – staring in God's face screaming with a bayonet on judgment day – ping that's the sniper – and God screams and puts the bayonet in – in the wounded belly – in the wha-wha – and theirs arms go up as if it wants to embrace – then fall back to its sides – and flap – like wings on a dead bird falling in the sky – and ours stops jabbing – theirs: a bit of blood pops from its mouth and dribbles down its chin – ours mutters as he wipes his bayonet on theirs jacket. God smokes. The fag still in his mouth. Didn't go out. I didn't understand my language.

FATHER. So what was all the fuss for! I knew that's what it was. I could've told you myself. Not the details but the gist.

Why couldn't you tell me before? You had a little war, mine was big. Don't blame yourself. And the lad with the bayonet – *he's* not to blame himself. Theirs should've understood: orders are the same in any language. It's us or them. In my war theirs booby-trapped their wounded. Put your hand out with a fag or can of water – bang! – it's blown off. Us or them. You look after your own. Thank God I've got Rene to care for. You'll find the wisdom of that when you settle down.

IRENE (*window*). Police car – end of the road!

BRIAN. – roadblock!

IRENE. He's waving up the street – they must be blocking the other end!

FATHER. They followed you. That's what I was afraid of. Tip off from the barracks.

IRENE (*bewildered*). You must've told them he had a gun!

FATHER. Rene – you make these accusations! I didn't phone! They didn't need my tip off! Did the barracks go to sleep?

IRENE (*to* BRIAN). Go through the back!

FATHER. No no Rene don't – that's not helping him! If I'd phoned – it'd be for his sake – to help him! Only for him! (*To* BRIAN.) They'll have men out the back – all over! Go with them like you said. Finish it now. I'll speak up for you. Please – no more.

Silence. They look towards the window but do not move.

IRENE. Quiet.

BRIAN. They're on the roof.

IRENE. If you'd gone I'd've gone with you. I wouldn't let you go alone!

FATHER. Rene – you make it worse for the poor lad.

BRIAN. Too late, too late. No one can help me. I went to the wrong place – saw the wrong things. This is the wrong place too. That's it: wrong – everywhere. (*To* FATHER.) You phoned! Admit it! (*Begs*.) At least that! What does it cost you! Why can't he tell me!

FATHER. You have your secrets, I have mine.

BRIAN. I could've walked to the station. Looked in the shops. Seen the sky. No one grabbing my arm.

FATHER. They wronged you when they put you in uniform. It's not for you. Not fair on the other lads.

The door swings open: half a policeman protrudes.

FIRST PC. Drop your gun!

BRIAN turns to the door – sees FIRST PC.

BRIAN. No.

A shot. BRIAN drops his gun. He stares at FIRST PC.

FIRST PC. Hands up hands up hands up hands up hands up hands up!

VOICES (*outside*). Hands up hands up!

BRIAN backs to the wall, stops when he reaches it. Silence. He lifts his hand. He puts his hand inside his windcheater.

A shot.

BRIAN's hand comes out of his windcheater – it shakes violently, red. BRIAN stares at the shaking hand. It sprinkles him with blood. Outside, voices gasp like a circus crowd. Silence.

BRIAN. Let me live. Let me live.

Suddenly the whole chest of his shirt is soaked in blood. He slips down the wall – leaving a red smear on it.

Immediately FIRST PC takes enormous strides into the room. An alsatian lollops after him. Then a crowd of policemen rushes in. They are misshapen, lumpen: armouring under their tunics. The policemen stand in a half-circle aiming guns at BRIAN.

SECOND PC. Watch – watch – trick – feign –

Pause.

SECOND PC. Search! Search! – Medics!

Chaos. The policemen scatter and search the room. Shouts, walkie-talkies, barking. Two uniformed legs descending in the window – FOURTH PC coming down from the roof. FATHER flat against wall. MEDICS with equipment enter.

FIRST MEDIC. What's his name?
SECOND PC. Brian!

THIRD PC *is holding* BRIAN *to the floor.*

FOURTH PC (*shouts down to the street through the window*). Ambulance – here – up – he's down – bagged!
VOICE (*from the roof*). Two shots!
FOURTH PC (*shouting up*). Ours!

The room – even more crowded. Medics. Stretcher. Oxygen and emergency equipment. The bed is upended. From outside the sound of police car and ambulance sirens.

FIRST MEDIC *puts the oxygen mask on* BRIAN's *face. In the chaos the alsatian licks blood from* BRIAN's *hand. Only* FATHER *sees it.* SECOND PC *stands astride* BRIAN's *gun on the floor – he has chalk and a tape-measure.*

SECOND PC. Mind – gun – want it right!

A NEIGHBOUR *enters with a young* CHILD *on her arm. A foot strikes the gun – it skews towards* BRIAN *and ends up by his hand.* FIRST MEDIC *is adjusting the oxygen mask on* BRIAN's *face. He stops, stares – at* BRIAN's *hand as it folds round the gun. He begins to back away. Slowly* BRIAN's *arm rises – the gun swings loose in his hand –* POLICE, MEDICS, *the* NEIGHBOUR, FATHER *stop – stare – slowly back away to the far side of the room.* BRIAN's *hand still slowly rises with the gun. His face is blank, livid white and partly hidden by the oxygen mask. Silence except for noise in the street. Some of the policemen shyly raise their guns. They stare at* BRIAN. FOURTH PC *crouches in the open window. The alsatian cowers and whimpers. Pause.*

The CHILD *climbs down from the* NEIGHBOUR's *arms. It*

crosses the space between the others and BRIAN. When it reaches him it stops. It chuckles and points its stubby finger at the gun. It turns to face the others. They stare back in silence.

CHILD. Look he give them – man give them –

Pause. Suddenly the NEIGHBOUR runs forwards, picks up her CHILD and runs back with it to the others.

NEIGHBOUR. Naughty – naughty – naughty –

Pause. The gun is slowly slipping through BRIAN's hand. It falls to the ground. The empty hand stays in the air, the fingers trying to grasp. The crowd lets out its breath. SECOND PC runs to BRIAN, throws himself on him, pinioning him to the ground, tears off the oxygen mask and hisses into his face.

SECOND PC. Yes? Yes? Yes?

The other policemen charge forward and pull SECOND PC off BRIAN. They start to scuffle amongst themselves. The medics replace the oxygen mask and attend to BRIAN. Unseen by the others a SENIOR POLICE OFFICER has entered. He stares at the scuffle and then turns on the NEIGHBOUR.

SENIOR OFFICER. Madam get out!

All the other policemen suddenly turn to look at SENIOR OFFICER. Moment's pause.

NEIGHBOUR (*to SENIOR OFFICER*). Know him – umpteen times – communal stairs – I'm a named witness –

The CHILD awkwardly pats the NEIGHBOUR's face with its fat little hands trying to gain attention.

CHILD. He give mummy – man give them –
SENIOR OFFICER (*furious*). Get out madam. (*Shouts through door.*) Who let this woman in? Put someone on the stairs! It's a sideshow! Chrissake give me some order!

The NEIGHBOUR tries to speak to IRENE and FATHER. She drops her shopping. Policemen pick it up

for her and bundle her out. As she goes she calls back to
IRENE *and* FATHER.

NEIGHBOUR. Are you all right? Anything you need?

IRENE *stands at the table. Her eyes are shut and her hands
are flat on the table top: it vibrates. She could be a clairvoyant
in a trance. A chain-and-bar ladder suspended from the roof
swings like a pendulum over the window.*

FOURTH PC (*to* IRENE). Are you all right miss?

IRENE's *hands are still on the vibrating table top. Outside,
sirens and cars coming and going.*

Miss? Miss?

PART THREE

The room milling with police and medics. BRIAN – the oxygen mask on his face, a medic injects his arm. FATHER wanders trying to find someone to talk to. IRENE stands at the table as before – her hands flat on the table top.

FOURTH PC (*to* IRENE). No harm now miss. It's over. I'll get a woman constable to attend to you.

The SENIOR OFFICER *is talking to* FIRST PC.

FIRST PC. Pointed straight at me.
SENIOR OFFICER. The second shot.
FIRST PC. Hand in his jacket – spoke couldn't make out what – swore straight at me – even when he was down. (*Turns to* SECOND PC.) You saw him with the gun.
SENIOR OFFICER (*pauses silently in suspicion, then turns to his second-in-command*). The ammunition could be cached up anywhere – they always have more than one weapon – coming here regularly – the girl wouldn't think – he'd hide it unbeknownst.
FIRST PC. Sir can a message be got to my wife and kids? – in case there's any rumours.
SENIOR OFFICER. His regiment's checking what's missing. (*Turns to* FIRST PC.) Good man.

FIRST MEDIC *checks the oxygen mask on* BRIAN's *face.*

SENIOR OFFICER *goes out to report.* SECOND *and* FOURTH PCs *stare at* BRIAN *and the medics.*

FOURTH PC (*to* FIRST MEDIC). Giving oxygen to butcher's meat.

FOURTH PC *goes to* FATHER.

FOURTH PC (*to* FATHER). You're being attended to sir. Your statement'll be taken at the station. Would you like to accompany the young lady downstairs? I presume that is your room sir is it? This sight'll upset her.

FATHER *wanders, trying to find someone to listen to him.*

FATHER. I warned them he was unstable. I saw his hand go in his jacket. How's your man to know? I'll put it in my statement. Quick reactions you lads. You know your job.

SECOND PC. In a minute sir!

FATHER (*goes to* IRENE). They're giving him the best attention . . . I knew this would happen. I had to call them: You can see he was out of control. The room could be full of bodies. If you'd let me call them before . . . A gun in a room like this – it takes over. You let yourself in your front door and five minutes later the world's turned upside down. (*He looks at* BRIAN *fear.*) That could be me . . . We'll get you another room to sleep in for tonight. It won't be easy to get back to normal tomorrow. God knows what it'll do to your exams.

IRENE. I thought the gun had bullets in it.

FATHER (*half attention, staring at* BRIAN). No no you're still in shock.

IRENE. I thought the gun had bullets in it.

FATHER. Of course you didn't. How could you tell? You don't know the first thing about guns. Can't even pull the trigger. It was the novelty of it: a gun in your hand – you were upset – so –. Now you feel guilty, accusing yourself for nothing.

IRENE. I thought the gun had bullets in it: he said he'd shoot you.

FATHER. No more. Please. I've had enough. I don't want to hear . . . You don't know *what* you thought. I've told you what happened. That's good enough for both of us . . . Let's go downstairs. I'll take you down. (*He stares at her.*) We're in enough trouble without this. (*Edge of craftiness.*) Anyone who had the nerve to try to kill would be smart enough to shut up about it in a room full of law. – You're a good girl trying to be too honest. It's natural you're confused.

IRENE. I tried to kill you.

FATHER (*compassion*). Poor Irene. (*Slight pause.*) You see it yourself: who knows what they do half the time? The policeman *thought* the lad was going to shoot him. He wasn't. And you think you tried to kill me. No no you lost your temper – for a tiny bit of a second. And luck has it there's a gun in your hand. If it'd been a cup you'd've thrown it. Instead you pulled the . . . your luck again: no bullets. A little tantrum doesn't mean you're a killer. Hardly meditated was it? We mustn't even think it could happen. What would it lead to? If we all judged ourselves like you, a room like this would turn into . . . (*Slight pause.*) It's like the man with the bayonet: you don't think he meant it? – it meant nothing. It was the situation. (*He stares at her.*) Sometimes I don't know what goes on in your head.

BRIAN *starts to breath stertorously. He is being strapped to the stretcher. The medics clear his throat with a suction probe. They connect him to a respirator – the hiss of its mechanical breathing is heard till he is taken away.*

(*To* IRENE.) Let's go down. This place will need decorating. All new. More expense on top of everything.
IRENE. I tried to kill you.

FATHER *stares at her then looks round in fear.*

FATHER. For Chrissake not here . . . (*Silence. Low.*) What are you telling me? You wanted me dead? Me there instead of him? Now? Is that what you want?

Silence. FATHER *starts to pull at a shirt button – the second one down from the collar. Tightly sewn. He grinds his teeth and tears it off.*

(*Low.*) Take it. Take it. I won't have it on me. You sewed it on. That's where people hang their lockets – chains – pictures they love – (*He puts the button before her on the table.*) Take it. You sit there and tell me these things. Your father. Take it. I won't have it. You touched it. Take it.
IRENE. I don't know now. I tried to kill you. It was right.
FATHER. Right? Is this a joke? You sit there and tell me it was right? Right? (*Bewildered.*) I don't know, I don't know,

I don't know. Is this something I've got to understand? Isn't what you've done enough – now you want to insult me? If I was dead – on that floor – you'd be spitting on what was left? (*He jerks at his sleeves as if he's brushing off spit.*) Put me under the floorboards? God knows what you'd be getting up to . . .!

IRENE. I tried to kill you.

FATHER. Stop it! You sit in this room and calmly tell me you –? It's not natural. Not human. He's dead because he got mixed up with you! You killed *him*! I know that! (*Calls.*) Officer!

THIRD PC (*crouched by* BRIAN. Looks up). It's all right sir we're doing all we can. (*Turns back to* BRIAN.)

FATHER. . . . I don't know what to do. Why have I got to cope with this? You're not well. You need attention. For your own sake. You could do terrible things. You must be put away. You sit there – all the time – day after day – fill in their papers: what's the use? How d'you answer their questions? What's two and two? I tried to murder my father. What's the – capital of Zambia? I tried to murder my father. Is that your world? Nothing makes sense any more. I don't know who we are . . . I don't care if it's true or not! If you can *think* it, it's as bad! Sometimes I'm not a good father. I lose my temper. Rage. No job. I can't give you the authority of a father behind you. But do I deserve this? I tried to make up for my faults. I loved you. I loved you. Took care of you.

IRENE. I tried to kill you.

FATHER. She keeps saying it! Is it a curse? What d'you want me to do? Why are you telling me?

IRENE. I tried to kill you.

FATHER. No no – I can't believe it. Never. Something happened to you – now you're scared – in a state. Are you trying to drive me mad? Is this the return I get? For a father's love? No. You're clinging to what happened as if this stubbornness justified it – was some way out. You're lost – you'll destroy yourself. We must stop now. Tomorrow will be different – if you get it right *now*. You under-

stand? Do it. Show me you understand that – want it – *now*.
Then you're not sick. I'll be content – let it drop. It can go
on as before: life – this house – can go on. We'll be wiser,
have more sympathy for all the little things that –. Start a
new way. No need to bring authority in. Do it on our own.
All you have to do is say you're sorry.

IRENE (*immediately*). No. (*Pause.*)

FATHER. She wants to pull all the buttons off! Then laugh!
Spit on me without these clothes! Write in it with her
finger! Then lick it to taste my pain . . . Tell me you're
sorry. For this. What you see now.

IRENE. No.

FATHER. You will say it. I won't take less. If you're not
sorry I'll open the ground under your feet and push you in!
They won't need to dig a hole. I'm waiting.

IRENE. No.

FATHER. I shan't wait long. I don't want to know what's in
your head. I don't want to understand. Knowing what you
are would damage me! Just say that word that's all. We'll live
by the rules. That's all you can offer. (*Harsh.*) Something
better may come of it. I hope so. Then we'll welcome it.

IRENE. I'm sorry.

FATHER. No. You're not. You say that to prove you're not.
That's the old answer: I murdered my father.

IRENE. I'm sorry I'm not a better daughter. I'm sorry I
leave clothes on the chairs. I'm sorry I put the lights on.
I'm sorry I don't study enough. I'm sorry I play the radio
loud. I'm sorry you haven't got a job. I'm sorry all day. I'm
sorry the world's what it is – and you've always been
unhappy. I'm sorry he's dying.

*The sounds of medical machines and from time to time the
engines and sirens of cars in the street. The* SECOND PC
chalks a line on the floor round the shape of BRIAN's *body.
From time to time other policemen come and go.*

FATHER. All right. I thought father and daughter were
close. When I was at the end of your gun I was closer to
you. I admit it: you tried to kill me. I saw it in your eyes.

Plain. They were more dead than the hole in the end of your gun. You had three eyes: they all wanted me dead. Yours more than the gun's, if the truth be told . . . I'm putting the button in my top pocket – see? – for you to sew on later when I put it out with the wash. It won't get lost. Mind you don't put it in the machine. They're hard on buttons. Break them . . . It's over, over, in the past. In a way you've set me free. Now there's nothing to pretend. We must go on. I have to live with you. There's still the problem of my job . . . I'm glad you're sorry for the other things. Now tell me you're sorry for today.

IRENE. No.

FATHER (*begging. Flat*). Please Irene.

IRENE. I can't.

FATHER (*withdrawn*). I'm beaten. You can see. I need you to tell me. Some reassurance. To help me to go on. I've been like this for years. End of the tether. Before you were born. I'm at the end. (*Sees his hands.*) I must cut my nails. Oh Christ. (*Pause*). I'm glad I'm not your child: I couldn't live in this world then.

The room seems almost empty. A few policemen and medics are left. BRIAN is carried out on the stretcher. The oxygen mask covers his face.

FIRST MEDIC (*explaining to* FATHER). Get the lad to another machine.

FOURTH PC (*turning in the doorway to* FATHER). Best here now. Crowded down there. I'll send the lady up.

FOURTH PC goes out and shuts the door. FATHER and IRENE are alone. He gets up and wanders to the wall where BRIAN fell. The chalk outline of BRIAN's body on the floor. FATHER gazes down – he is standing in the chalk outline. He crouches in the place where BRIAN fell when he slid down the wall, but with his forehead against the wall and his back to the room.

FATHER. They're never sorry. She said I'll take his money. He hides it in a suitcase. If I was dead they'd spend it now. Their loot. She isn't sorry. It's not in her.

FATHER *turns to face the room, still crouching. He picks up a broken end of chalk. He draws a line round his feet – the shape of his soles pressed to the ground.*

They won't like it. The powers that be. Dead people mustn't draw themselves. Anti the regulations on the use of chalk. This little piggy. I used to have a mother. Open the window if someone's there. This room smells of hospital.

IRENE (*opens the window*). I had to tell you. I wasn't angry. I can't tell you why I did it. I don't know the words: no one taught them to me.

FATHER. No more. (*Head on knees, peers up sideways, half-leering, half-crying.*) If I kill myself tomorrow . . . will you be sorry?

IRENE. It's your life. Do what you want. I'm not to blame. You shouldn't kill yourself.

FATHER (*stands*). Parents – children – say these things to each other . . . (*He gives a vague, loose kick over the chalk outline.*) I'm glad they shot the little coward . . . little bastard . . . let him rot in hell . . . in his room full of guns . . . (*He goes out.*)

IRENE *is alone. She shivers at the open window. She goes to the bed. She takes a grey blanket from it and wraps it round herself. She stands huddled with her back to the door.*

The door opens. A WPC comes in. She is in her late twenties, blonde, and ultra smart in an immaculate, close-fitting uniform. She has a shoulder bag. She looks at IRENE's *back and sees a huddled crone.*

WPC (*unsure*). Are you the daughter Irene?

IRENE *remains huddled, talking half to herself and half to the room. She is still shivering. Her face is livid and grey with weariness.*

No wonder you're cold. (*She closes the window.*) I've been detailed to look after you. A car will take us to the station. We've got a comfort room. You must see a doctor.

IRENE *mumbles a few words to herself. Tiredness has lowered and broken her voice.*

WPC. You've had an ordeal.

IRENE. He gave it to me. It was in my hand. I looked down at it . . . I've been so confused. They teach you this and that. I try to understand. Their confusion. They say it's a map. It's nothing, blank. Then I looked down – and the paper turned over – I saw – suddenly – clearly – the map's on the other side. I understood. There is a right and wrong, some things shouldn't be. It was right. Then. To do it. So I did. I pulled the trigger. And there were no bullets – I can't be touched. It's done. Now. Always. It's mine. I understood . . . it won't be like this all the time. The confusion will come back – it's outside the door!

WPC. They'll give you a social worker.

IRENE *stumbles slightly, shakes violently.*

IRENE. Food in the freezer – sew the buttons – in and out – crying – shouting – yah yah yah – (*Pulls the blanket tighter. The shaking changes to a tremble.*) But I saw. For a moment. I understood. I did it. It's mine. Always. When I'm old – look back – remember the people in the room – I'm sorry people are unhappy – but it will be different then – it will change – I know – it will be mine too – they will change.

WPC (*trying to understand. Glances at the papers on the table*). You're studying for your exams?

IRENE. . . . when I'm old . . .

WPC (*craning her neck forward*). Pardon I didn't hear.

IRENE (*as before*). . . . when I'm old . . .

WPC. You'll have to speak up if you expect me to hear.

IRENE *looks up. She has hardly been aware of the* WPC. She stares at her, raises her voice a little.

IRENE. . . . there was a child . . . it walked . . . (*Slightly louder.*) . . . walked . . .

WPC. A child walked?

IRENE (*looks down*). Away. (*Silence.*)

WPC. A lost child? You mustn't upset yourself any more today. You can't be responsible for everything. Someone's found it. Taken it to the station. It's home by now.

IRENE (*blunt*). The war. (*Twists round to face* WPC.) War.

WPC (*puzzled for a moment. Realises, guesses*). Ah – he told you –? They provide for orphans. The Welfare Authorities – Red Cross. They place them with families now. After they've been vetted and matched. They're very thorough. I bet it's in bliss. Children know how to cater for themselves. They make the most of what's on offer. (*No response.*) He died in the hall. Don't blame yourself. It's going to be all right. People get over worse. You don't believe me but I've seen it. What's wrong with your voice?

IRENE *looks at her. Then she goes to her, stops when she is close and gazes into her face.*

(*Stiff.*) Is anything the matter dear?

IRENE. Poor woman. Poor woman.

WPC (*drawing back, half-embarrassed, half-threatening*). Don't do that.

IRENE's *hand goes out to a plastic bottle of cosmetics on the table. She picks it up and thrusts it at the* WPC.

It's yours. Don't you want it?

IRENE. Take it.

WPC *takes the bottle.* IRENE *turns and walks away. Stops.*

. . . there's sand in my mouth . . . scraping my gums . . . the little boy's dead – the sand scraping his little bones . . . scraping the wind . . . Why? Why? Why?

WPC (*looking at the plastic bottle*). Good firm. (*Holds it up.*) Are you sure you don't need it?

IRENE (*to herself*). What day is it? I must lie down now. Sleep. Now. Tomorrow.

She lies on the bed, still wrapped in the blanket. She is young again. The WPC *stands guard at the window.*

Let me live. Let me live. (*She falls asleep.*)

The Rehearsals
The Dramatic Child
Famine

'The Rehearsals' was written for the Royal Court Theatre revivals of *Saved* and *The Pope's Wedding* in 1984.

'The Dramatic Child' was written for the Founding Conference of the International Drama and Education Association, held in Portugal in July 1992.

'Famine' was written for a benefit evening in aid of the former Yugoslavia held at the Duke's Playhouse, Lancaster, in February 1993 and first published as a broadsheet.

THE REHEARSALS

This story was told to me some years ago. It may be that my memory has forgotten some of the details and my imagination has added others. But the parts which seem untrue are not imagined and what I have forgotten are merely ordinary things that might occur in any story. Perhaps after all I have forgotten nothing. I wish to make this clear before I tell the story because the story is true.

Once upon a time there lived in a village a boy. When he was twelve soldiers came in a lorry and drove away with him and twenty other boys of about his own age, his friends and neighbours. The lorry travelled two days and a night. At regular mealtimes it stopped and the children were given army rations to eat. They arrived at a small town and were told to jump down from the lorry. Then they were formed into ranks and marched under guard to a large old house. It looked like many of the other houses in the town: built to shelter solid, middle-class, late nineteenth-century prosperity. The roof was grey-slated and the over-hang of the eaves at the two side ends was decorated with an ornamental wooden facia. The house had four storeys and, as they later found, a cellar.

The children were marched into the house. Inside were blind people seated on chairs in rows round the sides of the rooms with their backs flush against the walls or gathered into groups in the middle of the rooms. Others sat in the corridors or lay in beds or on the floors. A few sat on the sides of the stairways. There were no empty chairs. Perhaps there had been a store of them and one had been issued to each blind person as they arrived until the store was empty. The only people who could see in the house were the boys and their guards and a few orderlies.

The boys were told to wait. Almost immediately an official came into the house from the street. He wore a grey suit, an old, greasy, dark tie and an armband. He carried a stack of scripts. From his voice the children knew that unlike the

soldiers he belonged to their own nation. He told them they
were to rehearse a play which later they would act to a group
of visitors. They were to begin work immediately. The
children were pleased to have a play to act. They handed
out the scripts among themselves and started to organise
rehearsals. The blind people were silent. They did not speak
to each other or question the children. The old ones did not
even speak to themselves. All the same it was difficult to
rehearse with them there. They crowded the rooms and as the
actors were still only children no doubt they wished to put a
lot of running and jumping about into the play. They
explained their difficulty to the guards. The NCO went off
to see the official with the armband. After fifteen minutes the
NCO came back. The official had said the rehearsals were to
take place in the attic. They found this to be a spacious room
running the whole length of the house. It was well lit from
studio lights in the sloping ceiling and from electric lamps.
But the floor was covered by dead bodies and so again there
was a problem of finding sufficient free space in which to
rehearse. The NCO had said that the official had said the
bodies were to be taken down to the cellar. As the play was to
be performed in a few days, rehearsal time was short and so
the children were not permitted to waste any in carrying the
bodies down to the cellar. Instead the soldiers collected a gang
of blind people to do this. It was the sort of non-demanding
work they could manage. It was only necessary for the
soldiers to stand one blind person at the head of each corpse
and another at the feet. Then order them to stoop, grasp the
head or ankles and move forward. The soldiers organised a
file of pairs of blind people each carrying a corpse and led
them from the attic, winding their way on the staircase round
and round down through the house to the cellar while up in
the attic the children got on with the rehearsal of the play.

And the children enjoyed rehearsing it and later acting it to
the visitors. They couldn't understand the visitors' language
and noticed that some of them even seemed to be speaking to
the others in a language which was not their own so that they
stumbled over words and used more elaborate gestures than

they would normally have done. Children are very observant. All the same the play must have been well received: if it had not been they would have been told. And surely watching children act is always a pleasure?

Many of the things in this story may seem strange to us. It might seem strange to gather all the blind people from a wide area and put them together in one house. Wouldn't they have been better off and happier spread among the seeing community? It also seems strange that the attic should have been full of bodies. And strange that soldiers should herd together children and take them away from their homes and families. But none of these things seemed strange to the children. On the contrary they expected these and similar things to happen. It was what their experience of the world and indeed their learning had taught them to expect as natural. And they were very pleased to be taking part in a play. I do not know what it was called.

Later most of the children were killed by being forced to breathe gas. This also may come to seem normal to some people in some places. One of the children was not killed but survived in ways and for reasons that are of no relevance to this story. Many years later when he was well into middle age and indeed on the threshold of becoming old he was walking in a street in New York. He was not thinking about his childhood or, as he recalls, of anything very much at all – when suddenly he burst into tears. He stood where he was in the street, buried his face in his hands and his howls were heard above the noisy traffic of a metropolis. He had suddenly realised that the events in this story in which he had taken part were strange.

Edward Bond
1984

THE DRAMATIC CHILD

To whom may a child bear witness? To bear witness a child must itself be an authority. It has noticed something and intelligibly recounts what it has noticed. But it will give its account to another authority – to someone or others – who understand the account and who will act on it. This bridges the chasm between self and society. In bearing witness a child seeks understanding and justice. It tries to learn the values that give order to the world. To educate a child means to enable it to bear witness to its life.

There are two widely accepted – but false – beliefs concerning the upbringing of children. Really they are negative and positive versions of the same argument. The negative version is that a firmly disciplined child will grow to be a decent, law-abiding citizen; but a child will grow to be antisocial if its parents are not strict enough with it. A child trained in fear may conform – but fear produces obedience without the ability to judge, or cynicism with the inclination to opportunism. And obedience is the moralised form of cynicism.

The positive version of the argument is that a child loved and given security grows to be responsive, humane, considerate of others and able to act for a shared good. This version has clear advantages over the negative version. But it is not true that love and care enable a child to grow to be happy and considerate. It may become idly content – not given to brutal obedience but nevertheless unable to protect itself in a bad society.

Both these sorts of education do not develop the child's capacity to be critical. Above all, they do not allow the child to enter into the drama and tensions of its psyche.

It is necessary, here, to anticipate the end of the argument. Our present society changes rapidly and substantially. People need to become responsible for change, to understand and evaluate it and when possible to initiate it by anticipating necessity. Children must be helped to make change more human. To become competent members of a critical culture. This cannot be done by discipline, love or information alone – the child must enter with authority into its self-drama or become its own victim.

We need to understand what culture is – and our present cultural state. Western culture is replacing other cultures. Other cultures are as endangered as other species. In the past all cultures had to do two things: provide the means of existence and explain the meaning of existence – bear witness to life. The two things are closely connected. The economic and technological means of existence depended on forms of social organisation and ownership. These forms were necessarily also the authority that decreed the meaning of existence. A society's culture is the explanation it gives of itself. As human life is not static, culture had to maintain stability but also accommodate and legitimise change. When it could not, change was reactionary or revolutionary. All cultures had to accommodate conflict and tension or be changed by their inability to do so. Otherwise they could not provide the means of existence.

A child's natural state in society is conflictual. Its relation to the world is critical. It lives in a state of change, a dynamic flux which finds direction only by bearing witness. A child's psyche resembles society in its structural instability. This is not fortuitous. If it were not so we would live in evolutionary time and not in history. History happens because we are born in ignorance and have no instinctual place in society. Society is not a projection of instincts. Culture is an artificial, necessary contrivance. For history, technology (and its logic of development) are what chance and genetic mutation are to natural evolution.

A child's conflictual nature is not an extension of animal aggression. Indeed, it is our 'aggression' which prevents us from being animals. A child's conflicts are always a struggle over ideas, over the meaning of its self and of life. Animal aggression is always the attempt to maintain the status quo, to stabilise the state of the species. All human conflict is an effort to impose a new meaning on the world or to respond with new meanings to changes imposed by new technology. Again, this is analogous to the child's state. For a child, parents and other authorities are like the arrival of technology from the future; they impose new situations and demands (as technology does on the community) and the child must retain the integrity of its psyche yet constantly recreate itself in relation to these changes. This is the process of growing up. To the child, education is what history is to society – a means of recording and evaluating events so as to create a culture or character. However caring it is, the relationship between, on the one hand, a child, and on the other its parents and society, must be conflictual – just as history must. It might be possible for societies to create institutions that removed conflict from history, but the relationship of child and authority will always be conflictual – a strife of ideas – because children have no institutions. Children face the raw paradoxes of growing amongst signs of decay, of the weak among the strong. They become healthy by achieving wounds. This belongs to the drama of self that takes place in the social theatre.

Animals may depend on aggression because evolution (unlike history) is not the arbitration of ideas. Animal aggression is always mindless, action at the behest of instinct. Humans are never aggressive because even their violent conflicts are always an arbitration of meanings, the imposition of new meanings or the adaptation to old ones. The meanings are either the psyche's direct expressions or the responses to society's cultural meanings. These become part of the psyche, the way life is (or should be) lived. Though human conflict is a struggle for reason, it does not follow that meaning can always be arbitrated by reason. This is because cultural ideas are embodied in living practice with emotional and physical cognates. But (I repeat because it is important) this is not a human adaptation of animal instinct. Conflict divides us from prehuman animals and makes us creatures of cultures and ideas. We may call ourselves creatures but not animals because we are embodiments of our mind and we live our culture and its inevitable tensions.

It is important to understand the child's conflictual state. It has a will but it is not conceded autonomy and authority. Its mind is devoted to understanding the world – and its basic philosophical riddles – yet it does not have intellectual means to understand the world's structures and social relationships. It urgently needs evaluation but cannot wait for the facts. It cannot understand the world's dystopia. Essentially the child is bearing witness – recording the facts and seeking meaning for them. Many of the conflicts in the child's development have counterparts in society and history. The child must maintain its existence in a world others own. It lives on the sufferance of its good behaviour. It seeks understanding and meaning yet is in conflict with the forms of ownership that decree meaning. It asserts and adapts its will in order to become owner of itself. In societies this search for self becomes generalised, by the pressures of co-operation, into the development of democracy – and as time passes it gives new meanings to the word.

Achieving the means of subsistence required social ownership, and ownership of the means entails ownership of ideas and cultural ends. Yet all cultures are conflictual because society cannot fully represent the manifold psyches of its members: their roles are in conflict. And even if it could, the condition of childhood would make the adult psyche a source of conflict.

Culture legitimises the ways in which the means of subsistence are organised and owned and in doing so humanises existence, whether an existence of poverty or privilege. Paradoxically this does not mean that with the passing of time our actions become less barbarous. Our barbarism 'shrinks' but increasing technological power gives greater expression to the remnant. It is conceivable that when our species is at its most 'humane' its activities will be at their most barbarous and destructive. That is a paradox of modern technological civilisation. When the paradox is misunderstood it feeds back as the despair of 'high culture'.

Is Western society the highest form of humanisation yet achieved and is that why it erases other cultures? For a time

Western affluence provides the means of existence more
abundantly than traditional cultures can. But all cultures
need ideas which legitimise their economic systems and
which (in doing so) humanise culture and psyche. The social
means of existence can only be maintained by humanising
culture. But this is no longer so for Western affluence – and
that is comparable to a major mutation in our species. In the
West it is no longer necessary to create a culture and the ideas
which humanise and give meaning to life – it is only necessary
to maintain a system: the system of manufacturing, markets
and money. Western societies are the first human societies
that have dispensed with the making of culture. They depend
not on their ability to humanise and legitimise authority – but
on providing goods. They are societies of means without
ends. The system depends on markets and prisons; and
more and more of its institutions become types of prisons.
Now authority begins to use education to install the prison in
the psyche.

These claims are not rhetorical. Western affluence erases
other cultures because it is not a culture. It provides goods
without the struggles of the psyche to create culture. The
psyche's conflicts cannot be erased but authority can co-opt
them in intra-social anger and conflict. This reinforces the
negative state I have already described – the antisocial
conformity of obedience and discipline. Western 'anti-cul-
ture' colonises the artefacts and forms of the cultures it erases
– but in dehumanised ways, replacing tradition with fashion,
development with novelty, solidarity with charity. It assim-
ilates a culture by reversing its meaning – even to those who
created it. That is the secret of its power. It turns a force of
preservation and adaptation into a force of destruction.
Means without ends! The West's economic system is parasitic on the cultures of the past, on the cultures the system
destroys. It enslaves whole cultures and works them to death
. . . And what it does to other cultures it must inevitably do to
its own first source of cultural renewal: children.

Its children have nowhere to turn to bear witness. Their
conflicts have no counterparts in adult conflicts. The child

seeks meaning, adults struggle to maintain a system. The means have become the ends. Societies' artefacts are, now, not expressions of culture, demonstrations of its meaning, but merely things to consume. Objects lose meaning and become the toys of those who cannot play. Consumption replaces living. And machines think for us. The humanising tendency of the past is reversed. Society begins to become more barbarous.

We should not be nostalgic about the past and its confusions, sufferings, poverty and labour. That is not the alternative. But we live in a dangerous time. There is apparent consumer choice yet the system requires – compared to the past – an inappropriate level of conformity. The system must create inequality and (in any working society) this must create injustice – and in turn social tension. In response authority becomes more authoritarian and intolerant of systematic criticism. America allows free speech but empties words of their meaning. In America you can say everything and it means nothing. Narcotics, violence – even poverty – become sorts of consumer options. Social relations are dehumanised. Democracy becomes a form of tyranny.

That is the story of recent political history. Nonentities achieve great power. They introduce antisocial systems and call them reforms. Their spoken motto is 'there is no society'. Their secret motto is 'there is no culture'. In future – in the time of our children's adulthood – political mavericks will appear from nowhere – or to be precise, from the gutter or the bank. Their simplistic, reactionary programmes will do more damage to society. Then in their fear and anger 'democracies' will elect even more extreme and dangerous pseudo-saviours.

The child's conflictual needs will not be legitimised and developed by education, even in the concealed forms traditionally accepted by cultures. Education will be instrumental, adapting the child to maintaining the system. Conflict has always expressed itself in culture – the struggle over the meaning of 'being human'. Now education will deny a child culture – and thus strive to dehumanise it. The child may (though it may well not) be provided with technological gadgetry – and with the signs and artefacts of many cultures – but only in the superficial way in which the market exploits the exotic.

Education should enable children to search for meaning so that they may bear witness to life. The psyche is a dramatising structure and cultures are in a wide sense theatres. At first the child egoises the world, then anthropomorphises it – and then seeks personal and social meaning. It becomes a changing, embodied evaluation of the world.

The distinction between sport and art is revealing. Sport has often been of profound importance in culture. Maya ball games were literally a sacred matter of life and death – the losers were sacrificed. Now in the West sport is a matter of neutral skills to which enormous cultural, ideological and national significance is attached. Capitalism could not exist without sport. Sport arbitrates conflict on a fixed field according to fixed rules. It is used instrumentally while appearing to be cultural. This is not to deny the skills of sport and their aesthetic aspects. But mass sport becomes the site of violence precisely because governments and the market cathect it with cultural significance. Football 'hooligans' – even terrace racists – are disputing ideas with authority.

But drama is a game of no fixed rules. The point is to discover and create rules during the drama. Dramatic structures are unlike sport rules because the goals of drama are not defined as they are in sport. Drama searches for meaning and expresses the need to bear witness to life. Drama uses disciplines to define meanings, not take the place of meanings. And culture is essentially dramatic. It uses dramatic processes and expresses itself in dramatic signs. This belongs to humanising of our species. History and politics are transmitted through the psyche, and so culture is not purely superstructural but is – like the psyche – part of the material basis. When that is understood it can be seen why all culture is conflictual and can only be created in drama, not learned by rote, even when rote is practised as skill. A mind that could not recognise a story (and that means, being part of the story) would be mad. A psyche that cannot dramatise itself (and that

means, being an active part of social change) would be a
prison. Cultures always contest the division between the real
and the imaginary. It is one of the ways societies have access
to the material world. Drama is concerned with the tensions
of this boundary. In history the imaginary becomes real and
the real is consigned to the imaginary. There is conflict
between ideology and truth – and even a shared purpose of
madness and sanity. If the mind cannot enter – create – the
drama of these encounters, the encounters are acted out in the
real world of weapons and politics. Drama is not a substitute
for politics and does not do away with weapons. But unless
our psyches have access to the drama-of-the-boundary,
politics goes mad.

Perhaps Western affluence will maintain itself till it comes
up against the limits it itself creates. Then it will face the
scarcity and inadequacy that have endangered all cultures. In
the past cultures had the humanised resources to respond
creatively to these dangers. A dehumanised system would
not. It would have no creative cultural resources because its
'culture' is parasitic. It could respond only with discipline
and violence. So two problems face us. How to protect the
world from the market's ravages – and how to protect the
chance of cultural renewal and creation that children give us.
Their conflictual need creates knowledge and human-value
out of our material necessity. Children bear witness to our
humanity. We must help them to do this in ways that test and
legitimise their conflict or we dehumanise the future. Crises
would no longer provoke our strengths but find out our
weakness and destroy us.

For a time communities may exist without culture. It takes
time for their entropy to overcome the dynamic of the past.
But no child could exist without a need for culture: it is part of
a child's conflictual need. Yet education is so misunderstood
that we could use it to kill off the child's need. Whenever that
is done we fall into inhumanity and terrible things happen to
us. 'Being human' is not an instinctive thing, it is learned in
the psyche's drama. The future is threatened by a corpse with
a whip. The market's needs do not wholly represent human

needs: often they are in conflict with them. Education for the market's needs could be a prison. We must educate children for democracy. The psyche and society are a theatre or they are a prison. At the heart of all democracy is drama.

Edward Bond
June 1992

FAMINE

The wind said
Little child in your days
Ten thousand thousand breaths will enter and pass the gate of
   your mouth
I will blow the last breath away
I will scatter it east and west
To the north and south

The wind said
Little child under your skin four thousand bones
Are knit as cunningly as a spider's web
I will pick each bone clean
Like a vulture feeding on dreams
And scatter them in the garbage of war
I will make chaos
Like soldiers sharpening knives on war memorial stones

The wind said
Little child in your mouth are the sounds of a thousand pains
I will blow your shrieks over the city gratings
I will blow your cries over the frozen peaks
I will blow your sobs into the hollow plains

In what scroll is it written you shall die?
Little child I have blown the scroll into the empty sky
I have scattered the books of law
And the charters of state
For your grave I give you ruins
And for your pall hate
Cities have been laid waste
And armies lie dead
But no one gave you water to drink
Or a crust of bread

Edward Bond
12 January 1993

Interview with Edward Bond and Teaching Notes for *Tuesday*

Compiled by Jim Mulligan, who was, until recently, Head of English at Pimlico Comprehensive in London. He is now a freelance writer and Education Consultant.

INTERVIEW WITH EDWARD BOND

Tuesday is Edward Bond's second play for television and his first written for young people of 14–17 years.

When he was that age Edward Bond had already left school and was working in factories and warehouses in North London with little indication that he was to become a celebrated and controversial dramatist.

He had been evacuated to Suffolk and Cornwall but finished his formal education at Crouch End Secondary Modern School which he left when he was fifteen.

> I grew up in a world war so things tended to be disorganised, but in many ways it was an education in itself because one learned what it was like to be bombed. I remember little of my education but what left a great impression on me was the personality of the educators.

Some of his teachers were interested in regimentation and he tried to avoid that. The real educators were those who were generous enough to allow him to question. He was born into a traditional working-class culture and his parents, recently moved from the countryside, could not read, so there were no books at home and the books he got in school were:

> boring and patronising, about highwaymen and smugglers and the plays we were given to read, in a very working-class area, were totally remote, about public schools and going into the quad and doing prep.
>
> I did some writing at school and vaguely, at the back of my mind, I thought I wanted to be a writer. I was interested in words and, like most working-class people, was good at talking. Talking is drama so when I wanted a platform to express my ideas it seemed natural to write plays.

At that time all eighteen-year-old men had to do two years service in the armed forces and this is when Edward Bond really started to write.

I didn't like what I saw and I wanted to write about it. There was an atmosphere of violence and coercion. It was a very brutal society. Various ranks were given very unjust powers over other people and if you were an offender you could be publicly humiliated, degraded and brutalised. I saw in it an image of the society outside the army

Tuesday is a play that deals with the issues that Edward Bond has been writing about for thirty years: authoritarianism in families and society at large, the causes and effects of violence and war, and the impact of these on working-class people.

The play is about a soldier, Brian, who has gone absent without permission after his dreadful experience in a recent desert war. He is tormented by a memory of a small boy he saw in the desert and this memory is entwined with an experience when one of his fellow-soldiers bayonets a prisoner to death. Brian, armed with a gun, seeks refuge in the house of a girlfriend, Irene. She persuades him to give her the weapon and then, suddenly aware of the way her father has oppressed her, Irene attempts to kill him but the gun is not loaded. Her father then telephones the police who, thinking Brian is armed and dangerous, burst in and shoot him.

Edward Bond was asked to write the play by the BBC for the English File series.

I thought about what were the pressing problems and opportunities for young people and this is what I decided on. Obviously it fitted in with what I was writing and where my writing had brought me to. All previous plays prepare you to write the next play. I started working about six months before we filmed in the studio. I remember the story of the little boy who was lost in the desert suddenly popped up one late morning and I thought, yes, that's what I will write about. This is one of the central ideas. You could say there's this little boy in the desert who's running away from his parents. Compare that with the story of the soldier who is screaming for his mother as he gets bayonetted. Compare that with Brian who is shot in the room and compare that with Irene deciding to shoot her father. I want the students to think and feel about these images and compare them to our society.

It is a slow process of getting ideas. I work out very carefully what I am going to do before I write. I make lots of notes which are at least four or five times longer than the play itself. The actual business of writing always takes me by surprise and things that you thought were not going to be important turn out to be more important. I work every day from ten in the morning until seven in the evening. But, on the last draft, I can work very long hours, sometimes typing throughout the day and the night and I find it a great joy to do that although I don't keep it up for a long while. After the first draft I will do five or six drafts before the play is complete.

Originally I was going to say: the girl has this experience and then, when she's eighty, she looks back and talks about it. And then I thought: if I can't make this experience authentic to an audience in that room at that time then in some way I am not facing up to the problem. So in the end I set the play in one very small room and it all happens in 'real time' of one and a half hours. At the end of it you've got to feel that the girl is completely changed and that her life will be different after that. She has understood things that, at the beginning of the play, she did not understand.

Edward Bond acknowledges the enormous debt he owed as a young writer to George Devine at the Royal Court Theatre and Joan Littlewood at the Theatre Royal Stratford East.

I was just lucky there had been a break-through. If I'd been a writer ten years before nobody would have done my plays. Then working-class characters were either comic or part of the sub-plot. But at that time the Royal Court Theatre wanted young writers. The man who ran it, George Devine, said if there was anybody he should get rid of it was me because I would never write anything that could possibly be performed. Despite this he was very helpful. He couldn't understand a word I wrote because his training in theatre was entirely different. And yet, although that was his opinion, he did not base his actions on it.

Despite this support it was touch-and-go whether one of Edward Bond's first plays would be put on. *Saved* had a violent and controversial climax when some disaffected youths stoned a baby in a pram and killed it. When the writer refused to make cuts the play was banned, but still the Court put it on, trying to use a loop-hole in the law. They were fined by the authorities.

Edward Bond says he was surprised by the way *Saved* was criticised.

It would be immoral not to portray violence in plays. I find the mechanical violence in films and TV, the cult of encouraging people to seek personal revenge, very primitive and dangerous. If I show violence, it is always for it to be understood. It is not an end, never a solution. It is always a problem. I take violence and use it in such a way that for once an audience will be able to think about it in the context of the lives they are living and the society they live in.

I don't believe that being non-violent sets an example. You can be a child in the Gulf or somewhere and you can say: I am going to be non-violent. It doesn't stop somebody dropping a bomb on you. How would they know that you had made this remarkable decision? I am very much against war and violence. Violence is never anything other than force and that is very limited. It is never a philosophy, never a thought, but I can see situations where there is very little alternative to using violence. The one thing you can say about it is that it is legitimate when the weak use it against the strong but never the other way round. I was trained as a killer in the army but I have never killed anyone and I don't think I have ever been forced to use violence. When I was young I was exposed to a certain amount of parental violence. It was pretty customary then and I was assaulted by teachers.

When people say to me: you are exposing kids to violence, I say: when they get older they are going to be asked to vote for violence. I think it is legitimate for kids to ask why is it that adults are so violent.

I was once asked to give a talk in Coventry Cathedral, a sermon, I suppose it was. While I was thinking what to say I sat down in a kind of burger-bar. It was a summer evening and the place was full of families with their kids. In the short time that I was there I heard eight people say to children: if you do that again I'll kill you. And nobody paid any attention. I think it is legitimate for children to question that.

I think the future we face may be very bleak and the process of becoming less violent and more peaceful may be reversed. In the nineteenth century more people were beginning to realise that brutality by the state against the individual was a bad thing. It took some time to get there but they knew it was so. Now America is reintroducing the death penalty and the more affluent it becomes the more violent it becomes. My play is against all that.

Another central theme of *Tuesday* is the abuse of authority. In the play Irene has a flash of inspiration when she realises how much she is oppressed by her father and she attempts to kill him. Edward Bond wants this action to be understood.

I want my play to give the audience a sense of the practical, that if you make certain decisions, then you have to stand by them. Irene wouldn't say she was sorry. Her father would say: 'Come on. You don't entertain those thoughts in polite society. You learn to make excuses, to smile, to say the nice thing to authority.' But what Irene in effect says is: 'Actually, no. I don't want to do that because, in the end, if you do those things, you believe them yourself.'

I think, for a moment, she wanted to kill her father. This doesn't mean I want children to go around killing their parents and I don't want parents to go around killing their children even though it happens with astonishing frequency.

To anyone who says: 'Wasn't she lucky there were no bullets in the gun,' I want to say: 'No, wasn't the father lucky.' What I did in the play was apply a little trick. The gun happens to be unloaded but she doesn't know that and the audience doesn't know that. Therefore, the audience can go through this experience, can reflect on it and get new ideas. They can examine their emotions in relation to this thing and that makes the play useful to them. I am not saying: imitate that.

In his search for what will make society a better place to live in, Edward Bond does not see religion as a help.

I was terrorised by religion when I was young. I was told God so loved his son that he killed him. This seemed to be totally perverse. I remember being horrified by it, walking along the road and suddenly shuddering. It seemed bizarre and cruel. I think most children, when they are told this, must be traumatised in some way. It may be that it can be hidden, but religion is learning to be afraid. It is a very cruel idea that somebody should torture and kill somebody in order to save somebody else from something called sin. Murder is murder whether it is done by God or civilians or soldiers.

In recent years some theologians have even said that greed is good, it is good to be acquisitive. This means that we are living a basic conflict. Adults can't live by ten commandments yet children are expected to live by a hundred commandments and adults get upset when the children can't do it. You can't say: we'd like you to be acquisitive *here* but not *there*. It's like saying: we want the river to run in this direction here but will it just turn back there. Once you start releasing energy in a certain way, that's it. People can go to the Stock Exchange and make huge fortunes doing nothing and somebody else is expected to live quietly in apathy and poverty. We make young people cynical. Either they become cynical and opportunistic like many adults or they do what the kid in the desert does – they walk away from us.

Edward Bond would like his play to stimulate questions, to promote coherent thought and to help young people to be autonomous.

My play is written to take young people back to important basic situations and enable them to question what it means to be a human being. Young people ask very profound questions. What is the meaning of life? What is the meaning of the world? But later on they learn to ask how can I survive in my job? How can I pay my mortgage? Do I like my neighbour? The questions tend to get narrower as people get older. But there is a way of stopping this. There is always built into human societies non-conformity or the need to question. Not the need to believe. Lots of people believe mad things. I don't know of any mad questions but beliefs – there are many, many mad beliefs.

Education, at the moment, is trying to teach people not to question and if that happens we become dehumanised. Then the future is very bleak.

With *Tuesday* there are questions but no answers. Edward Bond is inviting the audience and readers to ask questions: the answers have to be worked out in their own lives.

TEACHING NOTES

I can't tell you why I did it. I don't know the words. No one taught them to me.

The language of this play may seem deceptively simple; there are very few difficult or dialect words. But what makes the text so powerful is that there are no wasted words. Let your attention slip for a few lines and you have missed something important. All the work in this section assumes that you have seen the video of *Tuesday* at least once and you are prepared to study the text so that you can think about some of the questions Edward Bond asks.

What's it all about?

To start with, discuss the following statements with someone. Try to agree on which statement sums up best what *Tuesday* is about and rank the rest of the statements in order of importance.

This play is about:

a) a boyfriend who comes between a father and his daughter

b) a young soldier deserting from the army only to be betrayed to the authorities

c) violence and death

d) a teenager who tries to kill her father

e) the way authority is used or abused in our society

f) people being responsible for their own actions

g) an unexpected violent incident that destroys a loving family

h) two totally unnecessary deaths

i) two young people who want to live but are prevented from doing so

j) a hardworking young woman whose life is ruined by her boyfriend and father

Peeling the onion: layers of meaning

When I'm old – look back – remember the people in the room –
I'm sorry people are unhappy

Who is the most influential character in *Tuesday*? Work with
somebody to rank the following people in order of importance:

> Irene, Brian, Mr Briggs (Irene's father), the boy in the
> desert, the prisoner who was bayonetted, any other char-
> acter

At one point Edward Bond thought of putting Irene's mother
in the play. What do you think about his decision to leave her
out?

Before studying a character you need to make a note of any
relevant references or quotations.
　Suppose you are going to give a talk on Irene. You might
decide to divide your talk into six sections:

- appearance etc.
- relationship with Brian
- relationship with Father
- Father's attitude to her
- Brian's attitude to her
- her new self-knowledge

Your first prompt card might be something like this:
Student
Mid-teens
Dress – skirt, blouse, open cardigan
We don't know what she looks like
Single child in single-parent family. No mother
More than one boy friend? – *I thought it was her other one*

Prompt card 2: Irene's relationship with Brian
　She puts her arms round him
　I won't jeer
　Was it my letters?

There's no one will hurt you
I'll go with you

Prompt card 3: Irene's relationship with her father
My father hides his money in his room. I'll steal it
You made him stare at your face. He's trying to sick your face up
He's my father. It's his house – implying that the father comes into her room if he wants
She sews buttons on his shirt

Prompt card 4: the father's attitude to Irene
Wait down like a good girl
You're not talking to Rene, even in my presence
Pathetic tart . . . my daughter's a tart
I can never trust her after what happened in this room
You're a good girl trying to be honest
If you're not sorry I'll open up the ground under your feet and push you in

Prompt card 5: Brian's attitude to Irene
I can't hurt you because you're kind
I can't live with you now
Then you took the gun like all the rest
If I told anyone – and they couldn't understand – jeered – I wouldn't want to live not even with you

Prompt Card 6: Irene's new self-knowledge
Go to prison if you want but I have to live here
I thought the gun had bullets in it
It's your life. Do what you want. I'm not to blame.
I was – for a moment I understood. I did it
There was a child. It walked away. The little boy's dead. Why? Let me live

There are many more references and quotations that you could use and, of course, all this could be used as the plan for a written character study.

Paths to production

The oppression of children by their parents is a theme Edward Bond wants us to explore. He is not asking children to go out and shoot their parents but he is asking us to think about the relationship between Irene and her father and to ask ourselves what we think she should do, or rather what we would do in similar circumstances.

Natalie Morse was at a state school in her final year of A-level studies when she had to decide whether or not to take two months off to play the part of Irene in *Tuesday*. She started acting for fun when she was six and had gradually built up a career alongside her ordinary school work, acting in adverts and films.

> I was really excited when I was offered the part. I knew it would be a challenge but it was going to be a wonderful experience trying to come to terms with the problems of this sixteen year-old. She was roughly my age and I believe what happened to her touches on the emotions of a lot of girls. Obviously it doesn't happen to everyone in the same way on one day but we have similar feelings and thoughts about authority and conflict and about the way you are prevented from doing what you know you can do.
>
> Irene had been silenced by her father and had never questioned his authority. I think all fathers have some of this authoritarian streak. I have arguments with my dad because he thinks his opinion is correct and he doesn't listen, so I've had to assert myself. But Irene had been silenced for the whole of her life and suddenly this door opened for her. She knew what the right thing to do was. There was no compromise for her. I've never had to open such a difficult door in my life because my parents ultimately have let me make my decisions but I had to imagine what it would be like to be totally oppressed.
>
> The interesting thing about *Tuesday* is the relationship between Irene and her father and I had to relate to both Edward and Bob in a kind of father/daughter relationship.

Edward was very supportive and would always discuss a problem without giving too much away. With Bob it was a much closer feeling. The characters were very hostile to each other but off the set he was nurturing and supportive.

It was a very demanding and emotional part. It was very hard to go away at the end of a day's rehearsals. For two months I didn't know whether I was coming or going. I was in an intensely dramatic situation and then I had to go home to my family and school friends and my A-level work. My parents will tell you I would come home emotionally drained and they had to take the brunt of it.

I didn't find it difficult to understand what Brian had been through. I understood that, when he talked about the boy in the desert walking away, Irene realised she could walk away herself. But the killing was another matter. I couldn't understand how a girl could kill her father and then one day Edward just told a story. He said it's like being in a lifeboat and he told the story. That was a revelation for me. It was so simple. The next day he had written the story down and from then on I had no problem with that critical scene. I understood that sometimes when you are in an unthinkable situation you have to do something which is unthinkable.

It was hard going back to school and examinations. It's not just coming to terms with the character, but the intensity of the experience. You have to know each other really well and rely on each other, so I do miss Edward and Ben and Bob, but in a deep sense Irene made me see things in different ways. She really opened my eyes to a lot of things. She is Edward's character but she will always be a part of me because of what I learned from her.

This is the story Edward Bond wrote for Natalie Morse to help her to understand more clearly some of the issues raised by the play.

The Plastic Water Bottle

A boat sank far out at sea. Six passengers survived in a lifeboat. Among them were a father and daughter. After drifting for three weeks the survivors had eaten their food. A plastic bottle of water was left.

They slept in shifts. Two survivors watched at all times. They kept watch in opposite directions. Between them they watched over the whole sea.

Each survivor took a sip of water at the beginning of each watch. Each drank six sips of water a day. They learnt that a sip may seem as large as an ocean measured in drops. Some of the survivors sipped longer than the others. They sipped with a deep intake that sounded like an angry hiss. Surely they were sipping more than their share?

The survivors were exhausted – on the margin of death. It was difficult to keep awake. They stood the plastic water bottle on the bench amidships. There it could be clearly seen.

Soon the plastic water bottle was half empty. One morning the girl feverishly drifted between sleeping and waking. The boat rocked. To her it seemed to be falling through space. Her limbs ached as if they were crushing her. She felt her mouth was like a metal funnel pushed into her face.

Her eyes opened a little. Her father was standing upright on the gunnel at the for'ard end of the boat? Half awake she wondered: why is father standing alone at the end of the boat? She saw that the bench amidships was empty. The plastic water bottle was in her father's hands. He had unscrewed the top and was raising the bottle to his lips. She realised he had gone to the end of the boat so that no one could stop him drinking. Had he been stealing the water – little by little for days? Was this the first time? The bottle had almost reached his lips.

Her eyes met her father's. She saw he was mad . . . she saw at once that he meant to gulp the water. His eyes glinted with dark spite. She knew that if he saw her raise the gun to shoot him he would throw the water into the sea. They would all die. But if she did not shoot him he would drink it and the rest of them would die even if he lived.

At the same moment she knew that she must shoot before he could drink the water or throw it into the sea. Yes now! She shot. The bullet went through the plastic water bottle. Two little jets shot out like a pair of horns. Wind was scattering the sparking water. Her father was stunned. For a second he stared at the jets. Would he try to drink the water or throw it into the sea? She knew she must shoot him. The other survivors were waking up like shadows rising in the light.

She shot him three times. He fell into the boat. The bottle fell on top of him. Bouncing a little. She jumped forwards. Picked it up. Water sloshed from the end and trickled from the holes. It wetted her dead father's jacket. She stopped the holes with her fingers. The other survivors stared at her – some staring even from their sleep.

A third of the bottle still held water. It lasted the survivors more than a week. Then one died. They decided to watch one at a time. The watches would be shorter.

The Father in *Tuesday* was played by Bob Peck who has acted in several Bond plays over the past twenty years and played Lear for two years in the Royal Shakespeare Company production at Stratford, the Barbican and on a continental tour. It was probably as a result of this that Edward Bond chose him for the part of Mr Briggs.

When Edward asked me to play the father in *Tuesday* I wanted to do it for him, to work with him, because of the quality and challenge of the writing and because it was for schools. Edward had a very clear idea of what the Father should look like and encouraged me to act in ways for TV that I have guarded against in the past. He wanted a heightened performance, you might say a theatre performance. In the past, when I've worked on Edward's plays, rehearsals would break down because we found the language impenetrable. We simply didn't know what the characters were trying to say or achieve. In a way I think he tries to make the characters say the unexpected. That doesn't mean he makes the characters inconsistent but it means you can never make any assumptions about any characters or their attitudes. They are shifting second by second and it makes you listen with complete attention. You can never drift off, either as an actor or as the audience.

When we were rehearsing *Tuesday* he would always try and get us to make decisions and make the exploration for ourselves. His very last resort would be to tell us what the meaning of something was.

The Father in *Tuesday* is a real character but he is not somebody you would meet on the street. He is a sort of distillation of a lot of people. To understand the character I try to bring my own experience to bear. I am a father and I recognise a lot of the man in myself. It's not just possessiveness – 'this is my house' – it's the temptation to use physical means and crude authority to get your offspring to do what you want instead of having a reasoned debate with them, treating them as equals, as human beings. This authoritarianism is very strong in parents and I think it is something this father has fallen prey to. It's the essence of his relationship with his daughter and in the play he's made to realise it's a sterile and dead relationship. In fact by the end he has no relationship and without it he is virtually dead. He's a walking corpse. All he has is his house.

It is a hard part to rehearse and play. We had more rehearsal before going into the studio for this than for any other TV play I have done and when we got into the studio we worked for twelve hours a day for over a week. They were very long days and it is very intense material: a man is held at the point of a gun by a young soldier he thinks is deranged, is made to go through a kind of mental torture and is shot at by his daughter. It is very highly charged and draining. When we were not actually on set recording, I would spend most of the time going over what was coming up, re-rehearsing in my head, rehearsing with the other actors or discussing with Edward what we should do. We would record a section of the play and then Edward would come down and give notes and try to move further on with an examination of the text. Even to the last take it was still work in progress.

Here are some lines which might focus your thinking about the father/daughter relationship.

> *You're not involving a girl her age. What sort of a father would I be if I encouraged you to do that.*
>
> *Stay down there. I'm not playing about. I don't want you up here.*
>
> *Am I supposed to lie in front of her? Your idea of a father.*
>
> *No work. The house needs attention. I'd like to afford Irene a few extras.*
>
> *If you look at me like that I'll put your eyes out. My God, I'm not a man of violence. I could take you outside and give you the thrashing of your life.*
>
> *I'm answerable to no one in this house. What I do in this place is right because I say so.*
>
> *I never rowed. We treated each other with respect.*
>
> *If I was dead on the floor you'd be spitting on what was left.*
>
> *Sometimes I'm not a good father. I lose my temper, rage. No job. I can't give you the authority of a father behind you. I tried to make up for my faults. I loved you.*
>
> *Is this the return I get for a father's love?*
>
> *In a way you've set me free. Now there's nothing to pretend. We must go on. I have to live with you.*
>
> *I need you to tell me . . . I've been like this for years.*

The father-daughter relationship is one theme in the play which you can talk and write about to help you understand the play and your own relationships.

- Hot-seat the Father and question him about his life and his relationship to his daughter
- Prepare a debate on the motion: By and large, parents do more good than harm
- Write an account, real or imagined, of a relationship between a parent and a teenager

Now make a similar study of another theme in *Tuesday* and treat it in the same way.

Every word you choose, every phrase you use: the drafting process

On 17 August 1992 Edward Bond wrote an outline of the play he was going to write:

> Teenage girl (*A*) has boyfriend in army (*S*). He's at war (Gulf, N. Ireland, Falklands or in some other colonial war).
>
> He comes back having deserted: because of seeing soldiers killing – they'd said they'd joined in order to kill but hadn't thought about it – said same sort of thing himself etc. Describes incident to girl. Wants her to put him up for a while. Doesn't want to go on the run.
>
> A's father (*F*) returns. Knows S has deserted? (local radio?) – argument – that S must do his duty – he's going to denounce S.
>
> S: Where's he going?
>
> A: Downstairs to phone.
>
> S pulls gun on F – will kill him. Argument moves to more profound level. S couldn't kill him – not unless it's to save his own neck – kill someone rather than to go to gaol for a few years etc. Hypocrite.
>
> A: You don't have to interfere etc. – don't have to know he's here.
>
> F: Duty.
>
> A: Both stop it.
>
> Tells S to give her the gun. A follows S down. She pleads with F that he'll destroy her relationship, she'll never forgive him etc. F more determined. Won't phone – instead going to the police station immediately. F goes to door.
>
> A aims at F. Pulls trigger. Click – gun not loaded.
>
> F: You tried to kill me!
>
> Shocked silence. F comes towards A. Stops. Click. Click. Click – she frantically tries to shoot F.
>
> F: You're mad.
>
> S could come in – he's been watching through the door? Waiting upstairs??

Leads to reconsideration of situation. All F can do is say: She tried to shoot me. S insists that weapons etc. change situations – that people find themselves doing terrible things before they know it etc.

F: Why did you try to shoot me?

A: I don't know.

F: But she meant it. She meant it. She tried to again – kept trying.

Could mother enter here?

S says here or later that he'd never put a bullet in because he'd never, never kill anyone.

F: Well your girlfriend would.

When S hears mother's voice he disappears rapidly back to A's room. Later she goes to kiss or hold him: he won't have anything to do with her because she's a killer.

Go through the first part of *Tuesday* and compare it to Edward Bond's synopsis. Work out what has been retained and what has been left out. Can you think of reasons for the changes?

Once the writing starts there is an evolution from a first idea, through many drafts, to the finished text.

What follows is an example of how Edward Bond worked on one tiny but crucial description. It is well worth studying how the language is changed and shaped: what is kept from the start; ideas that are dropped; the slight change in order to give a change of emphasis; the way the language is pared down and simplified so that the scene which is being described comes into sharp focus like a black and white photograph.

Get five different people to rehearse the different versions. Try to evaluate the dramatic significance of the changes that Edward Bond made and then make a presentation of the five versions giving a commentary explaining what you have found out.

Version 1

It was in the desert. We were quiet ourselves. The raids were still going on. You could see them flying over. We were quiet waiting for the order to go in a few days. They said stand down. The padre was singing hymns in his tent. I went for a walk. You can do that – slip away. You could even walk into no man's land. It was all our land really. Great big beef burger we're just waiting to put our teeth in. (*Sighs*.) I'm trying to tell you. It isn't much. I was in the sand. Dunes – little waves cut in them by the sea. Very regular, beautiful. Then here and there it's slashed open by a tank. A bloody great big steel machine dragging its grave round behind it. Little men hiding in the nets – camouflage. Ripped the dunes open – as if you could punch holes in the sea. And then it was flat. All those little bits of sand. Rock once. Little bits of silver grit. And then over there – quite a way off – I saw a bundle. It was white but dark. Gleaming and moving. I thought a mirage. But in war everything is unreal. You don't know what anything is any more. Unless you've got an order you shoot it or squash it. Then I thought, a little dwarf or a fat periscope under the sand.

Version 2

In the desert. Quiet. The planes were still raiding. See them going over. It made the desert quieter. We were waiting for the order to go in. Take a few days. Temporary stand by. I went for a walk. You can slip away though it's war. Into no man's land. I haven't got much to tell you. Don't expect much. Sand dunes. Littles waves on their sides. Regular. Really beautiful. Then where the tanks had slashed them open. Steel machines dragging their graves round with them. Then I crossed that and came to where it was still and flat. Flatter than the sky. All that sand. And I saw – some way off, I don't know how far? – a shadow moving. Black dot. I didn't see that thing above it that made the shadow. At first it was white – lost in the glare. Then I saw it was something walking in its own shadow as if that was a puddle. A mirage. In war you're part of a mirage. Or a periscope sticking up from the sand. I went closer. It was walking. A man. A dwarf.

Version 3

In the desert, in the quiet. Waiting for the order to go in. Temporary wait for a few days. Sitting. You can slip away even in war. Into no man's land. I went for a walk. I haven't got much to tell. I don't know if I can make you understand the sand. Little waves on the dunes. Regular, beautiful. Then the trenches where tanks had slashed them open. Machines dragging graves round behind them. Then I came to the still and flat sand. Flatter than the sky. I saw – some way off, how far? a shadow moving. Black dot. At first I didn't see the thing above that made the dot. It was lost in the heat. Then I saw something white was walking in its own shadow. A mirage. In war you're in a mirage. A periscope sticking up from a dugout?

Version 4

It happened in the desert. Temporary hold-up. A few days' quiet before the order to go in. Even in war you can slip away. It's not much of a story. I went for a walk in no man's land. Over the dunes . . . covered in long rows of neat little waves. Beautiful. Then where they're slashed open by tanks. Machines dragging their graves behind them. I went on. It was still. Flat sand, flatter than the sky. I saw – how far off? – a shadow moving. Black. Dot. First I didn't see the thing that made the shadow. It was lost in heat. Then I saw something white walking. A mirage? In war you're in a mirage. A periscope sticking up from a buried dugout? I got closer. Still walking. A man. A dwarf.

Version 5

It's not much of a story. It was in the desert. A temporary hold-up. A few days' quiet before the order to go in. Even in war you can slip away. I took a walk in no man's land. The dunes. Covered in long neat rows of little waves. Beautiful. Then where they'd been slashed open by tanks. Machines dragging their graves behind them. Went on. It was still. Flat. Sand. Flatter than the sky. I saw – how far? – a shadow. Black. Dot. A periscope sticking up from a buried dugout? No it was a moving shadow. First I didn't

see the thing that made it. Lost in the heat. Then I saw
something white. Walking on the shadow. A mirage? In
war you're in a mirage. I got closer. A man. A dwarf.
Walking in its own shadow.

Ideas for writing

One of the skills in talking and writing about a play is to refer
to things that happen (references) and to quote what characters say (quotations). You must be able to use quotations
and references to back up anything you say.

Some quotations can be used to illustrate more than one
point.

> FATHER. *Oh it's you. I thought it was her other one.*

This quotation could be used as evidence that Brian was not
all that special to Irene since she was going out with more
than one boy; or that Irene was, to use her father's words, '*a
pathetic little tart*', or that Brian was special to Irene and her
father was trying to make a cruel and petty joke.

Look at the following quotations. Decide who is speaking
and what the circumstances are. Work out how the quotations
could be used to support more than one point of view.

- *My father hides his money in his room. I'll steal it.*
- *Us or them. You look after your own. Thank God I've got
  Rene to care for.*
- *You're a considerate lad. Good at heart. That's why Rene
  took you up.*

Try to use short quotations and indicate either before or after
the quotation why you have used it. Here is an example of
how to use a reference and a quotation with an explanation.

I won't forget the child.
I went for the wrong
walk. I met myself.

This line expresses an idea
that is central to <u>Tuesday</u>.
The image of the child is
seared into Brian's memory.
He can hardly bear to speak
about it but when he does
he gives a precise and beautiful
description. He sees himself
as the child walking away
from the oppressive authority
of the family and state.
And yet, at the same time,
he sees the child growing
up 'into one of theirs to
kill us' or being found as
'a little skeleton with sand
in its mouth'.

Notice how the quotation is put on a separate line. There is no rule that says this must be so but it makes it easier to read the text. It also means that you do not need to use quotation marks. A useful rule-of-thumb is: if the quotation is only two or three words let it appear as part of your sentence using quotation marks; otherwise put it on a separate line.

After Irene has tried to shoot her father, Brian says:

> I'm like him. I can't live with you now.

In other words, by showing she is capable of killing, Irene has become like all the other killers that sicken Brian.

If you write about any of the following always base your ideas firmly on the text of *Tuesday*. Where appropriate use references and quotations and always use your writing to help you reflect on Edward Bond's ideas.

- The inquest into the death of Brian
- An interview with Irene at the age of 80
- Imagine the death of Brian is not seen on stage but is

recounted by Irene or the Father. Write one of the speeches
- Imagine the death of the soldier is seen on stage. Write the stage directions and dialogue
- Write a story based on the idea of the whole world being turned upside down by one unexpected event
- Write an extra scene showing the incident when Brian left the barracks

Just when you thought you had finished . . .

In a letter written after *Tuesday* was broadcast Edward Bond wrote about his concern that students should not concentrate only on the characters in *Tuesday*:

It would be useful to direct attention to the relationship between the room and the desert and the relationship between state authority and family authority.

He goes on to ask a series of questions:

Why does Irene feel it necessary to shoot her father? Why does the soldier carry an unloaded gun? Why does the soldier who has already killed say he will never kill? In what way is the girl with the gun different from the soldier with the bayonet? Is there a contradiction between the father's attitude to the bayonetting of the soldier and his reaction to his daughter's attempt to kill him? What is the play trying to make us experience and think about?

He concludes by saying:

I feel the play should help students to put their own immediate personal relationships into a wider context and to see how external authority uses private lives for its own ends. Irene discovers this and changes her life by making a stand against it. Otherwise protest becomes a matter of wearing too much make-up or having the 'wrong' sort of haircut. This trivialises protest and really is setting up a false quarrel with authority. It changes little.

METHUEN MODERN PLAYS

include work by

Jean Anouilh
John Arden
Margaretta D'Arcy
Peter Barnes
Brendan Behan
Edward Bond
Bertolt Brecht
Howard Brenton
Jim Cartwright
Caryl Churchill
Noël Coward
Sarah Daniels
Shelagh Delaney
David Edgar
Dario Fo
Michael Frayn
John Guare
Peter Handke
Terry Johnson
Kaufman & Hart
Barrie Keeffe
Larry Kramer
Stephen Lowe

Doug Lucie
John McGrath
David Mamet
Arthur Miller
Mtwa, Ngema & Simon
Tom Murphy
Peter Nichols
Joe Orton
Louise Page
Luigi Pirandello
Stephen Poliakoff
Franca Rame
David Rudkin
Willy Russell
Jean-Paul Sartre
Sam Shepard
Wole Soyinka
C. P. Taylor
Theatre Workshop
Sue Townsend
Timberlake Wertenbaker
Victoria Wood

METHUEN WORLD CLASSICS

Aeschylus (two volumes)
Jean Anouilh
John Arden
Arden & D'Arcy
Aristophanes (two volumes)
Peter Barnes
Brendan Behan
Aphra Behn
Edward Bond (four volumes)
Bertolt Brecht
(three volumes)
Howard Brenton
(two volumes)
Büchner
Bulgakov
Calderón
Anton Chekhov
Caryl Churchill
(two volumes)
Noël Coward (five volumes)
Sarah Daniels
Eduardo De Filippo
David Edgar
(three volumes)
Euripides (three volumes)
Dario Fo
Michael Frayn
(two volumes)
Max Frisch
Gorky
Harley Granville Barker

Henrik Ibsen (six volumes)
Lorca (three volumes)
Marivaux
Mustapha Matura
David Mercer
Arthur Miller
(three volumes)
Anthony Minghella
Molière
Tom Murphy (two volumes)
Peter Nichols
(two volumes)
Clifford Odets
Joe Orton
Louise Page
A. W. Pinero
Luigi Pirandello
Stephen Poliakoff
Terence Rattigan
(two volumes)
Ntozake Shange
Sophocles (two volumes)
Wole Soyinka
David Storey
August Strindberg
(three volumes)
J. M. Synge
Ramón del Valle-Inclán
Frank Wedekind
Oscar Wilde

METHUEN STUDENT EDITIONS

Annotated plays intended for students at home and abroad

Alan Ayckbourn
Confusions

Aphra Behn
The Rover

Edward Bond
Lear

Bertolt Brecht
The Caucasian Chalk Circle
Mother Courage and her Children

Caryl Churchill
Top Girls

Shelagh Delaney
A Taste of Honey

Henrik Ibsen
A Doll's House

John Marston
The Malcontent

Harold Pinter
The Birthday Party
The Caretaker

J M Synge
The Playboy of the Western World

Oscar Wilde
The Importance of Being Earnest

Tennessee Williams
A Streetcar Named Desire

METHUEN YOUNG DRAMA

A range of new plays for young people – as audience or participants – drawn largely from the work of professional writers and theatre companies

Richard Cameron
Strugglers
(winner of the Sunday Times Playwriting Award
at the National Student Drama Festival in 1988)

F K Waechter/Ken Campbell
Clown Plays (School for Clowns, Clowns on a
School Outing, Peef)
(written to be watched by 8–12 year olds)
Skungpoomery
(written to be performed and watched by 7–12 year olds)

David Holman
Whale
(originally written for the National Theatre
in 1990 for 7–12 year olds)

George Orwell/Peter Hall
Animal Farm
(with music by Richard Peaslee and lyrics by
Adrian Mitchell)

Willy Russell
Our Day Out
(with songs by Bob Eaton, Chris Mellor and
Willy Russell adapted from the television play
and written for the Liverpool Everyman Theatre
and staged there and at the Young Vic, London 1983)

Sue Townsend
The Secret Diary of Adrian Mole aged 13¾: The Play